TEACHING
the GOSPEL
TODAY

TEACHING the GOSPEL TODAY

A Guide for Education in the Congregation

MARGARET A. KRYCH

AUGSBURG Publishing House • Minneapolis

TEACHING THE GOSPEL TODAY
A Guide for Education in the Congregation

Copyright © 1987 Augsburg Publishing House

Scripture quotations unless otherwise noted are from the Revised Standard Version of the Bible, copyright 1946, 1952, and 1971 by the Division of Christian Education of the National Council of Churches.

Library of Congress Cataloging-in-Publication Data

Krych, Margaret A., 1942–
      Teaching the Gospel today : a guide for education in the
   congregation / Margaret A. Krych.
         p.   cm.
      Bibliography: p.
      ISBN 0-8066-2295-4
      1. Christian education.   I. Title.
   BV1471.2.K75 1987
   268'.6—dc19   87-28999
                                                                                     CIP

Manufactured in the U.S.A.   APH 10-6226

1   2   3   4   5   6   7   8   9   0   1   2   3   4   5   6   7   8   9

*To Arden, Meredyth, and David,
who have taught me so much
about communicating the gospel.*

CONTENTS

PREFACE

For some years the question of communicating the gospel has concerned me. Especially the research in cognitive development in recent decades has deeply challenged me as it has so many Christian educators. In teaching in the local parish myself, and in preparing seminary students to face that task, I felt compelled to seek ways of teaching the gospel that neither ignored cognitive development nor delayed teaching until well into the teenage years. Watching children struggle with concepts beyond their grasp, seeing young people leave the church in the teenage years, and hearing adults confess that they never really understood what Christianity was about when they were young, convinced me that new approaches had to be sought by which the gospel could be communicated to persons of all ages. The discovery of a tool and a methodology that were helpful in teaching the message of justification by grace through faith was the joy of my doctoral studies at Princeton Seminary. It is out of this experience that this book came to be written.

Throughout, the reader will be aware of my great debt to theologian Paul Tillich, in whose writings lies a passion for communicating the gospel and a methodology for teaching which have not been sufficiently tapped for their richness and vision. Tillich is well known in all denominations for the depth and breadth of his theological work. But he deserves also to be recognized as a religious educator of great insight. In addition, the work of Professor James Loder of Princeton on the transformational process has been exceedingly influential in my search for a tool with which to communicate the gospel. Dr. Loder's advice on the dissertation project was of incalculable benefit.

One of the moving experiences of my life has been the teaching of the gospel message using the methodology that is described in this book. I have found it to be a breakthrough in my own teaching, and hope that it may be of some benefit to others who, like myself, seek to communicate the good news so that learners may hear the Word and respond in faith.

Chapter 1

PROBLEMS
IN COMMUNICATING
THE GOSPEL

Ll of us, no doubt, would like to be able to communicate the gospel clearly. But it isn't always an easy task. There are many reasons for this difficulty. Following are some of the most common that teachers encounter today.

The irrelevant news

"How was Sunday school today, dear?" asks Mrs. Anderson.* Ten-year-old Lynn shrugs her shoulders. "O.K., I guess. We learned a lot of stuff about someone or other who lived a million years ago." Mrs. Anderson smiles. "Well, it can't be all that bad. I'm sure a million is an exaggeration. And what you learned must have some value for you." Lynn replies, "You've got to be kidding. I got the answers in the crossword puzzle right, and that's the closest this class comes to having any value for me. But don't worry—I'm polite, and I don't yawn much."

Lynn's situation is only too common, unfortunately. We may present accurate biblical material and stories about wonderful

---

*The names used in the illustrations of teaching situations in this book are fictitious.

saints of the faith. But, unless the good news is presented in a way that touches the actual lives of the learners, the news received by the learner is really far from *good*. In fact, it may be entirely irrelevant. Learning of the faith of others long ago is only valuable if today's fifth graders grasp the relevance of faith to their own lives and respond personally to God as the Lord of life in the schoolroom, the playing field, and the many other activities in which they are involved on a daily basis.

Too often, teachers present the gospel as relevant for people in the past, or for a child's future life as a teenager or adult. They may assume that children easily make the transition from someone else's experience to their own. But, in fact, children need help in relating the good news of Jesus Christ to their everyday existence.

Nor are children the only learners who may fail to perceive the gospel as relevant. Despite their increased cognitive abilities, adolescents still do not readily relate the good news to their daily lives without a teaching methodology that enables them to do so. And neither do adults.

Consider John at 15 who, after years of Sunday school and catechetical classes, cheers delightedly at the prospect of sleeping in on Sunday mornings now that he no longer feels pressured by parents to "have to go to church." Or Ivis at 18 who wishes that she knew how memorized Bible facts might help in dealing with the grief of losing her boyfriend to her best friend. Or Duane at 26 who feels bitter that church classes have never prepared him to face the tragedy of a young wife dying of leukemia. Or Joanne at 39 who lives a dichotomous existence with no relation between her "Christian life" defined as Sunday and Thursday evenings and the rest of her life as a corporate executive. Or Peter at 55 who is growing tired of "passing the faith on to others" when it seems that it has little to do with approaching retirement. Or Lucy at 80 who suspects vaguely that she doesn't believe all that she was taught about faith and death but feels that at her age she shouldn't be exhibiting too many doubts. The list could go on indefinitely. The fact is, that if in teaching we merely tell about the faith of our forebears—and even witness to our own faith—but fail to help the learners make the association between their own lives and the good news, then we have failed genuinely to communicate the gospel. The gospel is essentially a message crucial to the existence of believers. If the learner is able to grasp the relevance of the gospel for his or her daily life, then it may not be so very terrible if he or she forgets most of the "material" the teacher has tried to present! The most important learning will have occurred.

In the following pages, a methodology will be suggested that will help communicate the gospel in a way that is perceived to be relevant by the learners. It isn't the only way to teach the good news. But it is one way, one method, that works in the classroom—and the pulpit and in one-on-one situations as well. It is a method that works with children, youth, and adults.

The partial news

"I think the most important aspect of teaching is helping our students have faith," says Bob at the teachers' meeting.

"Well, of course," agrees Tina. "I make sure my students can repeat the Creed word for word in the first four weeks of my class."

"I don't think repeating words is having faith," cries George. "It's feelings that matter. I want to make sure that my students really feel right about God. A warm feeling in their hearts is far more important than reciting correct information."

"Feelings aren't enough without commitment," argues Sandra. "I tell my students, 'You have a will and only you can yield that will to the Lord. You must voluntarily make a decision to follow Christ.' That alone is faith in my opinion."

The difficulty in this conversation is not a difference of aims on the part of the teachers. All are agreed that their primary goal is to teach in such a way that their students may have faith. The difficulty is theological. In Paul Tillich's terminology, these teachers are guilty of distorting faith by reducing it to either a matter of cognitive information, or emotional response, or volition. Tillich points out that faith is a total act. "It is not an act of one's volitional, emotive, or cognitive functions alone. Faith is an act wherein all the elements of one's personality are 'synthesized' and 'transcended.' The act of faith embraces such elements (volitional, emotional, cognitive), raising them to a higher unity without being identified with any of them." [1] In other words, faith is partly volitional but is never purely volitionless nor purely volitional. It is also partly emotive, but can never simply be reduced to any sort of feeling—no matter how warm! And, faith is also partly cognitive, but cannot be reduced to purely a matter of the intellect or of remembering information whether creedal, biblical, or any other kind. To reduce faith to any of these functions is to be guilty of distortion, and any such distortion is to be rejected. [2] Instead, faith must be understood as an act of the whole person in which the person is centered in an act of personal commitment.

As teachers, we are constantly faced with the temptation to reduce faith. Our very efforts to define goals clearly, so necessary in teaching, may even foster this temptation. If we can formulate a simple measurable goal, such as, "To have the students repeat the Apostle's Creed twice without a mistake," we may be inclined to think that our work is on the right track. But simply to equate such an activity with "having faith" would be to make a serious theological error.

On the other hand, this does not mean that the teachers holding the above conversation are totally in the wrong either. None of the functions—intellectual, emotional, volitional—can be discarded. Tillich says of the intellectualistic, voluntaristic, and emotionalistic distortions of faith, "Such interpretations are not altogether wrong because every function of the human mind participates in the act of faith." [3] In other words, there is a dialectical complexity in the role of intellect, will, and emotion in relation to faith. As teachers, we cannot ignore the intellectual or emotional or volitional aspects of our students. But neither can we separate them and allow any one of them to be identified with faith. We must not present the gospel as a list of beliefs to which the learner must subscribe, nor a set of feelings the learner must have, nor a command to believe. Rather, the gospel must be presented as a message in which God grasps persons in their totality, in a response of utter dependence and trust that involves the whole person. We shall say more about faith in the following chapters, as we explore methods of communicating the gospel in ways that address the whole person of the learner.

News for children too

"I am so frustrated," cries Josephine. "I feel like giving up teaching Sunday school altogether. Today is the first Sunday after Pentecost—the festival of the Holy Trinity. So I wanted to teach the class about the Trinity. But do you think that I could get my children to understand what I was trying to teach? I might as well have been talking to the wall."

"Maybe it was your big words—or perhaps you didn't have enough activities that interested them," suggests Terry. "After all, anyone can learn about God as Father, Son, and Holy Spirit if you teach in the right way."

"Perhaps not," says Pastor Johnson. "I have tried teaching seventh and eighth graders about the Trinity and, frankly, I haven't felt that I have communicated successfully. I find that most kids don't have much notion of what I'm driving at until the end of eighth grade or even well into ninth or tenth grade. And somehow I don't think that simple words or different activities are the solution. But I have no real answer. To be honest, I'm not sure if it is me that is the problem or if it is something to do with the kids themselves."

Probably no issue is more confusing for teachers at present than communicating in ways appropriate for various age-levels. Particularly at issue is what to teach on the cognitive level. Presenting biblical or theological material used to be thought a fairly easy task—if one could find simple words, then persons of any age were presumed capable of understanding the ideas being taught. Psychological research in recent decades has radically challenged this assumption. While the gospel can never be reduced to merely cognitive propositions, as we have already made clear, nevertheless, there is a cognitive component to the communication and reception of the good news. Research in cognitive development, therefore, has important implications for religious educators in helping them decide what may be grasped at particular age-levels and what is better left for some other age-level. First, it may be helpful to summarize the findings in the field of cognitive studies, and then return to Josephine, Terry, and Pastor Johnson.

Prior to the work of Jean Piaget, most educators—including religious educators—treated children as miniature adults. Beliefs were presented to children in the same way in which they were presented to adults, although with shortened sentences and simple words. But the world-wide studies in cognitive development that began with Jean Piaget and then were continued by post-Piagetian research in many countries through the last few decades has shown that children's thinking is qualitatively (not merely quantitatively) different from that of adults. In fact, children develop through a series of stages in their cognitive development to the point where (at about eleven-or-twelve-plus years) they are capable of "abstract thinking" (that is, the kind of thinking that is typical of adults).

Piaget proposed that intellectual development develops in a series of stages that are invariant for all children. The actual ages at which stages appear may differ from child to child, depending on genetic endowment and environmental quality.[4] In this sense, Piaget's theory includes both nature and nurture, both heredity and environment.[5] As a matter of fact, in most children, the stages appear rather closely related to age.

Piaget's theory lists six stages of intellectual development.[6] The first three are sometimes grouped together since they all involve sensory-motor experience. These are the reflex or hereditary stage (birth to one month), the stage of first motor habits, first organized percepts, or first differentiated emotions (one to six months), and the stage of practical or sensory-motor intelligence (from six months to approximately two years).[7] Few churches have programs of a cognitive nature for these stages. Therefore, church school teachers tend to have most concern about stages four, five, and six.

The fourth stage Piaget calls the preoperational stage. (Sometimes it is divided into two substages—preconceptual thought from two to four years, and intuitive thought from four to seven years.) During this period children develop abilities that have to do with representing things (the elaboration of the symbolic function). They use words as symbols, remember the past, and make-believe. Their thought is often distorted because they try to make reality fit their own desires and because they reason from particular to particular rather than from particular to general or vice versa (as adults do). Because preoperational children cannot reverse their thinking, they cannot check their reasoning and so their thinking is often nonlogical from an adult point of view. Also, their thinking is centered—they tend to focus on one part of a problem and ignore other parts, thus failing to consider the relation between the parts or between the parts and the whole. Young children, then, reason in a way that is decidedly different from the teacher.

Children's minds are not passive recipients. Actively involved, children try to make sense of anything they hear. This may well result in distortions and misapprehensions of many biblical ideas. All the good teaching in the world cannot force young children to comprehend that which is beyond their intellectual capacity. Their brain cells just aren't developed to the point where they can reason like adults.

The fifth stage Piaget terms the stage of concrete operations. It lasts usually from seven to approximately 11 or 12 years of age. Concrete operations are really internalized actions that permit the child to do mentally what previously would have had to be accomplished by real actions. Children in the concrete thinking stage can think about things and the relations among classes of things.[8] Their thinking is no longer centered; they can focus on

17

the interrelation of parts and wholes. And their thinking is reversible: they can check their mental reasoning processes and so are capable of logical reasoning.[9] They conserve quantity and number, and develop concepts of movement, speed, time, and space.[10] They are able to see the point of view of others, and their ability to generalize develops during this period. But children in the concrete stage are still limited to thinking about those things which in principle are perceivable through the senses; therefore they give a sensory referent to every concept, including those concepts which do not have sensory referents from an adult point of view. (For example, "spirit" will only make sense to the child as something that could literally be touched, tasted, smelled, heard, or seen.)

The last stage, commencing somewhere around 12 years of age, is typified by the emergence of formal operations or logical thought or abstract thinking. Formal operations allow persons to deal with abstract constructions, to use symbols for other symbols, to construct ideals, and to reason about the future. Persons in the abstract thinking stage are able to use complex reasoning, apply principles in theory, and consider propositions about situations that are contrary to what they know to be factually true. They are able to introspect, to think about their own thinking, and to envisage how they and their ideas appear to others. They can deal with global generalizations, grasp metaphor, and think about things which are not perceivable in principle through the senses.[11] Most of these aspects of thought are necessary for mature theological reasoning. No new stages or mental systems emerge after formal operations: abstract thinking is the way in which normal adults think.[12]

The research in cognitive development has resulted in further studies in stages of moral development[13] and religious conceptual development.[14] Ronald Goldman, using Piaget's stages of cognitive development, found consistent patterns of religious thinking which exemplified the late preoperational stage, the concrete stage, and the stage of abstract thinking.[15] Typical of the stages is the way in which children view God. For the preoperational child, God is seen in purely physical and human terms.[16] In the concrete thinking stage the child is still limited to describing God in physical terms but looks for some special attitude that makes God different in some way from human beings. Toward the end of the concrete thinking stage, the child gradually conceives of God as having a superhuman quality.[17] And finally, in the stage of formal operations or abstract thinking, the young adolescent conceives of God in abstract and spiritual terms.[18] Goldman holds that personal religious thought is not well-developed and the child is not capable of mature doctrinal thinking until 13 to 14 years of age.[19]

And so we return to Josephine, Terry, and Pastor Johnson. Josephine correctly perceives that she is not communicating abstract conceptual material to her students. Terry's well-meaning guidance is really not helpful. Monosyllables do not make the idea they express any the less complex. And interesting activities will raise the student's motivation but will not decrease their frustration at having to struggle with understandings that are beyond their grasp. Pastor Johnson senses this, but, like many teachers, is not sure whether to blame himself or the students. Actually, no one is to "blame"; neither the teacher nor the students are "the problem." The students are merely developing in the wonderful way in which God intends; their development is part of creation and, as such, is good. A problem arises only when the teacher feels that children ought to reason as adults while their brain cells are still developing toward adult maturity.

Well, then, what should the teacher do? Ronald Goldman proposes religious education built upon the concept of "readiness." Readiness in any field of education assumes that there is a time in development when the maturing of a child allows learning to occur that was previously impossible; that there are incremental stages in learning a skill which must be systematized; and that we can assist the process of readiness by suitable preparatory learning.[20] Goldman believes that religious education requires intellectual, emotional, and physical readiness. Therefore, he recommends that biblical and theological content should not be presented to children until they have the mental capacity to comprehend fully the concepts in the way in which the (adult) writers meant them. Teaching of theological and biblical material should, in Goldman's view, be delayed until the child is ready for it. Thus much theological and biblical content will not be taught until religious formal operations have been attained at about 13 or 14 years of age. Goldman argues that teaching too much of the Bible too soon has dangerous consequences—children gain incorrect understandings that later must be unlearned, and children become bored since they cannot understand what is being presented.[21]

While coming from different points of view, many others have wanted to support the idea that the teaching of theological content must be limited on the basis of behavioral studies in the field of cognition. We might consider James Fowler's more recent proposal of the development of faith in an invariant sequence of stages. In Fowler's scheme of six stages of faith, the period of infancy through two years is termed a *prestage* prior to faith. The intuitive-reflective stage (corresponding to the preoperational stage of thinking) is a time when persons appropriate faith "by examples, moods, actions, and stories of the visible faith of primally related adults."[22] In the mythic-literal stage (concrete thinking), story is the major way of giving unity and value to experience and faith is communicated by narrative, drama, and myth.[23] In this stage, the child is incapable of "reflective conceptual meanings" of stories; the meaning of the story is "trapped" in the narrative and cannot be released for the child.

Such thinkers force us to ask the question of whether it is possible to take the child's development seriously and still communicate theological concepts or major doctrines of the Christian faith in a meaningful way to children while maintaining theological integrity. Should Josephine and Pastor Johnson simply give up their desire to teach theological content to their students under eighth grade?

This question is a crucial one for teachers of religion today. Some choose the easy solution of simply ignoring research in cognitive development; they go on teaching children as if they were miniature adults. This results in frustration for the students and is an insult to the Creator, implying in effect, "Lord, you made a mistake! Children really should be able to reason as adults do." Others, as we have seen, suggest delaying the teaching of most theological concepts until adolescence.

For the teacher who honestly desires to take development seriously and yet communicate the gospel, including cognitive aspects, the issue can be an agonizing one. What if Josephine responds, "But isn't there any tool by which some central theological teachings can be communicated to children? Can't I take the child's development seriously without delaying central issues such as sin, grace, justification, and faith until adolescence?" As we develop a methodology for communicating the gospel in a way that is relevant for the learners and addresses the whole person, we shall explore a tool by which to communicate some cognitive aspects of the gospel without violating children's development. This tool is of particular value in the church school classroom since it can be used easily by most teachers. There may, of course, be other tools, some still waiting to be discovered.

News for all ages

"Thank goodness I teach adolescents," mutters Brian as he listens to Josephine, Terry, and Pastor Johnson.

"And I'm glad I have adults," agrees a seminarian. "At least with students at our age levels we can simply give them the Bible and expect them to understand it. Teaching abstract thinkers is by far the easiest job."

"I wish you'd tell me how to do it then," says Sally. "I've taught both youth and adults at various times. Believe me, young people's ideas can be as peculiar as those of children. Sometimes you feel that you are un-teaching most of what they have learned previously. And then, when you do get the students going on the right track they often seem to take two steps forward and three backward in the learning process. And as for adults . . . they are so diverse. Some seem to think like children and others are so far ahead I feel that they ought to be teaching the class instead of me. When you add to that their diverse interests and life-styles, you have a very heterogeneous group. I don't see what's so easy about teaching adolescents and adults."

Sally's point is valid. If the gospel is to be communicated to all age levels, we must take account of the most appropriate ways to communicate to youth and adults as well as to children. As a matter of fact, what we do with children will have profound implications for what we then do in teaching adolescents. Similarly, how we teach adolescents will have important implications for ways of later communicating to those persons in the adult years. In coming chapters, as we explore methodology and tools for communicating the gospel to children, we will also consider building on children's learning into youth and adulthood so that we may teach in a way that takes account of developing intellectual maturity and increasing diversity of experience.

Chapter 2

A METHOD
FOR COMMUNICATING
THE GOSPEL

We have seen the importance of communicating the gospel in a way that is perceived to be relevant by the learners. Now we need a methodology in teaching that enables the learner to grasp the gospel as God's action *for me*. Of course, in using any method it is crucial that first we who are teachers grasp that the gospel is indeed *for us*. As the old adage has it, faith is caught rather than taught. A method will be helpful only in so far as it helps communicate a gospel that the teacher already deeply believes. Learners quickly perceive a teacher's own lack of commitment. But, if we have commitment, we still need a way or a method of sharing with others the news which means so very much to us personally.

A method of correlation

Where can we find such a method? It will be helpful to consider some major thinkers who have wrestled with the question of methodology in communicating the gospel. In particular, we shall draw on the insights of Paul Tillich. Tillich believed that the best method for communicating the gospel is actually inherent in the gospel itself. He took seriously the central message for the Reformers as that of God's merciful forgiveness of the sinner—or, another way to put it, God's answer to the human question of sin. In other words, a question-answer pattern is to be found in the gospel: the *question* of sin and the *answer* of God's action on our behalf in Jesus Christ. We shall explore further the matters of sin and God's saving acts in the next chapter. At this point we shall examine the pattern or method—a pattern that is essentially relevant since it begins with the learner's own need and then moves on to show how God's action is answer to that very need.

Tillich used many disciplines—philosophy, poetry, drama, psychology, sociology, and so on[1]—to help in illustrating and analyzing the questions in the human situation. And the way in which the answers to the human questions were expressed took account of the analysis of the questions. But the substance of the answer, Tillich believed, must always remain the same since the answers can only be derived from God's revelation, from the gospel.[2] The content of the answer must be provided by the Christian message of Jesus as the Christ. So then, the answers cannot be inferred from the questions, but the questions will help to shape the form of the answers. In other words, the hearer will be able to see that God has not answered problems that do not exist but has provided direct answers to the human needs which he or she has.

Tillich believed that the answers to the deepest human needs can never come from philosophy or any human discipline; only revelation is able to go beyond the "structure of being" manifested under the conditions of existence with its contradictions, incompleteness, conflict, distortion, and ambiguity. Our human existence is itself the question—it can never provide the answer. Only revelation can disclose the ground of being which is unconditional and give us genuine answers to our deepest human needs. The answers of the gospel to the questions in the human situation, therefore, are inevitably spoke *to* our existence from beyond it.[3]

When teaching the answers contained in the revelatory events, Tillich directs our attention to the sources of theology which are the Bible (the basic source), church history, and the history of religion and culture.[4] All of these will be important in our educational task. These sources speak to us through the medium of human experience.[5] Our experience should not change the central message, the revelation in Jesus Christ. But teachers' experiences will color their presentation of the message and learners' experiences will affect their interpretation of the message.

Tillich reminds us that, in presenting the message, we should always keep centrally focused the criterion or standard by which to guide our use of the sources and of our own and the students' experience. That standard or norm was expressed in the 16th century as justification by grace through faith—or, as Tillich prefers to express it in the 20th century, reconciliation or reunion which overcomes our self-estrangement. And this reconciliation or new creation or "New Being" is manifest in Jesus the Christ.[6] In Christ we see the answer to the question of our human situation. Reconciliation through Christ then must be central in all of our teaching.

Tillich thus believed that a method of correlating the answers of the gospel with the questions implied in human existence was the correct way to approach theology.[7] And he also went on to say that this was a pattern that teachers and preachers could use in communicating the gospel—a practical method which would ensure that relevance was built into the communication from the beginning. Indeed, Tillich felt that correlating the answer of the gospel with the questions in the human situation was *the* best method for those who seek to communicate the gospel.

A law-gospel pattern

The pattern of correlating human need and divine revelation in theology is not a new one. Martin Luther's theology, with its law-gospel pattern, was a Reformation understanding of the law which served to reveal to us our sin thus driving us toward and opening us up to the message of the gospel. Luther distinguished between gospel and law but nevertheless held them in a creative relationship. The Reformers understood both law and gospel as the work and the Word of God, and both as necessary in proclaiming God to the sinner.[8] However, they clearly distinguished the law as message of rebuke and condemnation and the gospel as promise of forgiveness of sins for the sake of Christ by grace through faith. While salvation is through the word of grace and not the law, nevertheless it is the chief function of the law to drive the sinner to the gospel. The gospel will not truly be received as the Word of comfort unless the law has already brought the hearers to a knowledge of their true state before God. And the law will be understood correctly only when the gospel is known. As Christians, we stand under both law and gospel; we are both sinners and saved simultaneously. Thus we need to hear both law and gospel, and neither can be proclaimed without the other.

Paul Tillich's method of correlating questions and answers reflects a similar complex interrelationship[9]—the answers of the gospel cannot be perceived as relevant without the analysis of the question which reveals to the hearer his or her true state of existence. But the question cannot provide the answer: it can only point forward to the answer. Question and answer are to be clearly distinguished and yet the two are interrelated. The formulation of the question takes account of the answer of God's activity on our behalf; and the expression of the answer is done in the light of the human question. The hearer's human situation must thus be taken very seriously if the gospel is to be communicated effectively.

Other writers too

Other writers in this century also argue strongly for the necessity of taking the human being seriously where he or she is. Rudolph Bultmann, for example, suggests that, by using a set of categories, we can put the appropriate question of human existence to the Bible. By putting the appropriate question to the Bible, the answer of the gospel can be received in a way that informs the hearer who she is and enables her to structure her life upon that answer, to enable her to become in reality a new person.[10]

Contemporary scholar Gerhard Ebeling also argues forcefully that, for the gospel to be heard, the human situation must first be analyzed in terms of its "questionability" to which the answer is the gospel. In today's secular society, Ebeling believes that all of us experience the ambiguity of existence, the questionableness of ourselves and of reality. The horror of world events is one way in which that questionableness is brought home to us and we ask, "Where is God? Is he absent?"[11] To such deep-seated questionableness at the heart of the human situation, the gospel of God comes as good news, the news of God who imparts himself to us and opens up for us a future of freedom.

Currently, the writing of David Tracy has renewed interest in a pattern of correlation.[12] Tracy seeks a reformulation of the meanings present in common human experience and those present in the Christian tradition.[13] Theology, for Tracy, involves a critical correlation of the results of the investigation of these two sources.[14]

For our purposes, it is not necessary to analyze in detail these writers. Nor do they all say exactly the same thing. But, the important thing for us as educators is to note the pattern they suggest—first, taking serious account of the human situation and then correlating the Christian message with the human situation.

The method in Christian education

All of the above thinkers were talking about a way to approach theology. But as we have mentioned, Paul Tillich went on to suggest that the way in which we approach theology can also be a method for practical purposes.[15] In preaching and teaching, Tillich suggested, we should follow the same pattern that the theologian follows in developing his or her careful elucidation of the good news in Christ. First, we should deal with the learner's questions and then correlate the answers of the gospel in appropriate ways so that God's answers are grasped as good news, relevant for the learner.

Ten-year-old Lynn, in our Chapter 1 illustration, failed totally to perceive that the information she was learning had anything to do with her life, her situation, her questions. Her sole participation in class consisted in repetition of irrelevant information, such as completing crossword puzzles accurately. While such activities may have given Lynn a little sense of satisfaction, she saw her role as basically fulfilling directives politely. We could say that the teacher had failed in communicating both question and answer to Lynn. A correlation method would call for a different approach in which the teacher would deal with the deepest questions in Lynn's existence, help Lynn realize who she is and what she needs, and see the answer to those questions in the new quality of reconciled life manifested in Jesus Christ. In a correlation approach, teaching about people long ago is only of value in so far as the stories help Lynn to perceive her own situation and God's answer for her own life. In other words, the criterion for choosing lesson content will be its value in genuinely communicating God's good news to the 10-year-olds in Lynn's class.

In dealing with the good news for Lynn, we should not foster an individualized gospel that neglects community. A method of correlation used properly should help Lynn appreciate that her fellow students share her deepest questions. And so does the teacher. And so do all human beings, although the questions may be experienced in different ways and expressed differently. Lynn should sense that she is not alone in her questions. And she should learn that she is not alone in receiving the answer. The good news is shared within the church community and calls us together to share and struggle, to suffer and rejoice, as we hear and respond to the Word in worship and as we witness and serve. Christian education, therefore, consists in introducing "each new generation into the reality of the Spiritual Community, into its faith and into its love."[16] Such incorporation into the community of believers has been important from the earliest days of the church. From the reception of the first family into the Christian church long ago, the church has had an educational function, the task of receiving new generations into its communion.[17] And this function is still critically important today.[18]

Tillich calls teachers to help students come to a conceptual interpretation of religious symbols without destroying the power of the symbols. Such help in interpretation is a crucial aspect of Christian education. On the other hand, Tillich warns against giving the traditional symbols before the pupils are ready to deal with them.[19] But, once the first "critical questions" are asked by the child, then the first cautious answers must be given; as the child grows older, the questions become more critical and the answers more fundamental.[20]

The ideals of education

In pursuing this correlation approach in Christian education, Tillich believes that we shall fulfill the ideals of humanistic and inducting education. "*Educating* means leading out from something."[21] If asked leading out into what, humanism would reply, "into the actualization of all human potentialities." But under the conditions of our finite existence no one can fulfill the humanist ideal since only some of the potentialities can be fulfilled in some of the people. Inducting education, on the other hand, has the aim of induction into a group—the life and spirit of community, family, nation, church. The ultimate aim of induction would be initiation into the mystery of existence, but instead in our world we induct into a finite society or group or denomination.[22]

Tillich holds that the solution to fulfilling the ideals of humanistic and inducting education lies in using the correlation method in religious education. The church school must find the existentially important questions which are in the hearts of the pupils and then show that the traditional myths and symbols of the Christian message were originally conceived as answers to the questions implied in human existence itself.[23] Not only does this fulfill the induction process in a meaningful way but it deals with the humanistic question since in Jesus the Christ all human possibilities are opened up so that learners may develop in freedom.[24]

29

TEACHING THE GOSPEL TODAY

Education in the Spirit

Tillich recognizes that Christian teaching in the churches is always tainted with what he calls the ambiguities of life.[25] We work toward the growth of a student—and at the same time run the danger of depersonalizing the student by treating him or her as an object to be manipulated.[26] We try to find a middle way between letting the student go ahead without any guidance and controlling the student by indoctrination. In our world we are always caught by such conflicting dilemmas.

However, Christian education has hope in a way that secular education does not. This is because, in the church, the teacher and learner are able to be grasped by the Spirit of God in whom all the ambiguities of life are overcome. In the grasp of the Spirit, the attitude of superiority and will to control the student can be replaced by the acknowledgment that the teacher is in the same predicament as the learner.[27] Teacher and learner can thus mutually share together in the learning task and respect each other. Similarly, in the home, only the Spirit can deal with parents' doubts that Jesus is indeed the Christ and give them courage to affirm his lordship and communicate it to their children.[28]

Of course, Christians are always simultaneously both saved and sinful. The experience of being grasped by the Spirit is only fragmentary—teacher and student, parent and child, are both caught and under the conditions of sinfulness and under the impact of the Spirit. Therefore, we who are teachers and parents are called to be humble, continually confessing our doubts and our self-serving, as well as prayerfully trusting in the Spirit to guide our teaching.

Some important factors

Tillich suggests factors that make for ease or difficulty in communicating the gospel so that persons are able to make a genuine decision for or against it. One helpful factor is that, despite the place and period in which a person lives, despite variations of environment, there is always something within the human situation that is constant, and that is the starting point of the method of correlation—the human predicament, with its structures of anxiety and conflict and guilt. These structures mirror to us what we are. To bring these structures before people is to hold up a mirror in which they see themselves.[29] However, just because we hold up the mirror does not guarantee that persons will in fact see themselves as we hope. Teaching is a risky business with no guarantees of success.[30]

A second factor that affects genuine communication of the gospel is what Tillich terms *participation*. In order to teach effectively, we need to participate not only in common human existence but also in the particular existence of our students since this deeply affects the way in which the questions and the answers are expressed. People today are diverse in background and outlook. They may be used to asking questions to which the gospel is not the answer. They may have rarely if ever heard the gospel before. They may feel bitterness because of the way they have been treated in society. They may have ethnic concerns that we do not understand. If we cannot understand the learner's situation, it is unlikely that we can teach the gospel effectively. Because to be effective we need to get in touch with the questions in the hearts and lives of the students; then we can help the learners formulate those questions in ways that are more applicable to the gospel answer.[31] Only then can the gospel be perceived as relevant.

As teachers, for example, we need to participate in the situation of our students in the sense of understanding their particular ways of experiencing estrangement, anxiety, and guilt. We cannot simply transfer our adult experience on to children or teenagers and expect the students to recognize themselves. Tillich thought that, in one sense, teaching children may be easier than teaching adults since children do not have so many years of education and of formulating the wrong questions to which the gospel is not the answer.[32] On the other hand, there is the inherent difficulty of participating in the children's situation to the extent that we can genuinely deal with the children's own questions. We adults often attempt to give answers to questions that have never been asked by children, or phrase the answers in abstract terms and concepts which are beyond their grasp.[33] Taking the learner's own existence seriously means taking account of degrees of maturity, of sociological and psychological factors that affect our students, and so on.

Of course, it is not our task as teachers merely to respond to the surface questions which our students may express verbally. In the classroom we shall be looking for the deep "question marks" of existence that cry out for answers. Such questions must be analyzed and interpreted in the light of the gospel answer. God has answered our deepest human needs and we must ensure that the deepest existential questions are genuinely those dealt with, rather than dealing with merely secondary concerns that children or youth or adults happen to express. The deepest questions are, in fact, the same existential questions which are typical of the whole human race of whatever age, but they are experienced in particular ways in early childhood, and in later childhood, and in early adolescence, for example, which must be taken account of when teaching.

A method of correlating questions and answers requires a certain openness and flexibility on the part of the classroom teacher. Students may be at quite different points in the "formulation" of the questions, and need more or less help in moving toward asking the appropriate questions. The teacher is called to be sensitive to each student in order that the gospel may genuinely be communicated to each individual. In itself, this is asking no more than any good educational approach would recommend—namely, that education should be learner-centered rather than subject-centered and that all content and methodology should be adapted to the needs of the individual learner.

Presenting both "question" and "answer"

We have suggested that built-in relevance can be achieved when a lesson begins with the students' own situation and moves on from there. And that this pattern is reflected in content—*what* we say—as well as in methodology—*how* we go about structuring a lesson plan.

This does not mean that every class session must have two precisely equal parts any more than a sermon should have exactly ten minutes of *question* and ten minutes of *answer*. It does, however, mean that some careful thought must go into planning a session so that appropriate time and steps are allotted to exploring the *question* side of the correlation and also the *answer* side. In some sessions more time will be given to the question than in others. For example, if there is an aspect of their situation that students find difficulty in expressing, or that calls for pouring out of feelings, you may want to allow considerable time for the exploration of the question so that students are not hurried and the question is clear. In other sessions less time will be needed for the question—perhaps it will be a deep longing that is readily recognized and you will feel the students almost panting for the good news; you will move on faster. Similarly, more or less time may be given to exploring the answer. The most important point to keep in mind is that the answer must be given with sufficient time to be received as genuinely good news. To teach law without gospel is not good news! No matter how gripping the analysis of the question—and adults particularly sometimes enjoy belaboring their experience of the human situation—as teacher you need to ensure that the answer is given and correlated with the question so that learners leave rejoicing in God's action for us in Jesus Christ. To leave students hanging by promising them that "next week we shall get to God's answer" can be emotionally damaging—even assuming all the students will be present next week, which is often not the case. But even more, to present *question* without *answer* is untrue to the gospel. The law should point us to Christ, not merely to itself. Our task is to communicate the good news, and the analysis of the question should be seen as an important step in doing that, not an end in itself.

TEACHING THE GOSPEL TODAY

Teaching from the Bible

It may sound as if starting with the human question means never starting a lesson with the Bible. Not at all. Law and gospel are both aspects of the Word of God and both are found throughout the Scriptures. On many occasions the Bible can be the most fruitful starting place. It is full of gripping illustrations of the human condition and can be a clear mirror that shows us who we are. In Chapter 4 we shall use biblical narratives for both question and answer.

Sometimes you may find it useful to begin an analysis of the question with an illustration of the human question from some other source—drama, novel, videotaped story, audiotaped song, poetry, illustration from medicine or psychology, passage from a philosopher's writings, or whatever seems most appropriate to the age level. In this case, do not lose sight of the scriptural analysis of the human situation. A contemporary illustration is helpful in so far as it interprets in readily-recognizable terms the biblical understanding of our fragmented, sinful condition. On the other hand, if the contemporary illustration fails to incorporate an essential aspect of the biblical insight—for example, fails to emphasize our human responsibility for sin—then you will need to draw on the "basic source" of theology and add the missing insight. Contemporary illustrations should be used to elucidate the biblical understanding, never to warp or minimize it. No matter how fascinating or motivating you think that a film or record may be, if it does not truly reflect all or a helpful part of the biblical view of the human question, then it should not be used. Be especially careful in choosing illustrations to use with children. Adults may more readily hear our warning that the attractive teaching aid or illustration needs to be corrected and will view it accordingly. Children will often remember the illustration and forget the important corrective that you felt should be added.

Similarly, in presenting the answer, we must ensure that it is presented in a way that is true to the biblical witness to the Christ. Our task is to present Jesus as the Christ in whom all the ambiguities and estrangement of life are overcome and thus the one who brings true healing and newness of life for us. The Scriptures will be our basic resource. Insights from the history of the church will help us. Any contemporary teacher-aid must be scrutinized for its transparency to the gospel message so that students may hear the good news and respond in faith to Jesus as Lord and Savior.

Sample session

Following is an outline of a typical session plan that incorporates the correlation method. Bear in mind that this is a sample only. You can draw up any number of plans of your own with the use of different procedures. But be sure to retain the correlation pattern of question and answer.

Sample Plan for Lynn's Class

1. Singing and psalm of praise (to start on a positive note)

2. The Question
    Story Part 1—Peter's Denial and Need of Forgiveness
        (John 13:36-38; 18:15-18, 25-27)
    Class development of playscript on Peter's denial
    Group discussion—what Peter might have felt and
        thought after the denial
        —a time I've felt like Peter
    Labeling the feelings—words we use in church
3. The Answer
    Story Part 2—Peter's Restoration and Commission
        (John 21:15-19)
    Continuation of playscript on Peter's restoration
    Group discussion—how Peter might have felt when
        Jesus gave him a new start
        —how we ask for forgiveness and a new start

4. Brief Review of Question and Answer (to cement the
    correlation)

5. Group reading of the play the class has developed

6. Centers—
    writing center: write a poem about Peter's experience or your own
    puzzle center: make up your own puzzle about Peter and try it on a friend
    prayer center: write a prayer for your own use or to use in class; tell God about your experience and how you feel
    art center: make a mobile; on the shapes write words that remind you of Peter's experience or your own
    Bible center: read the story of Peter in the Bible

7. Sharing time—sharing what was done in centers, emphasizing correlation of question and answer

8. Prayer and Praise including prayer for forgiveness and song of praise to our forgiving God

Chapter 3

THE GOSPEL TODAY

In order to teach the gospel effectively we need to examine our grasp of the central message of the Christian faith. The Reformers believed that justification by grace through faith was the "main doctrine of Christianity,"[1] the doctrine by which the church "stands or falls,"[2] the central message to be proclaimed.[3] Justification has been central for the Reformation and its present-day heirs and also for much 20th-century ecumenical theological conversation.[4]

But how are we to express God's justifying or rightwising activity on our behalf in terms that make sense to learners of various age-levels in today's world? Terms change their meaning over the centuries. Words that are familiar in one era sound strange and unfamiliar in another. Phrases that are common in a Christianized era sound foreign in today's secular world. We need both to tell the good news in a way that is true to the scriptural witness and also in a way that does not leave hearers bewildered by terms and ideas that they do not understand. And, we need to present the good news in a way that is relevant for the learners and engages them in the totality of their being. This is a large task! But, unless we attempt it, we shall not be able to communicate the gospel effectively.

The question

We said in the last chapter that, for the gospel to be relevant, it will need to be perceived as the answer to the human question.

Or, to be even more specific, your students need to perceive the gospel as answer to their question—and their deepest question is that of the whole human race. It is the question of sin. To start at the beginning, therefore, let us consider the "bad news" to which the gospel is answer.

It is always helpful to have a measuring rod against which to check what we say. From this angle, we can ask what the 16th-century Reformers said about sin. Then we can consider how we might need to "translate" that understanding for today's children, youth, and adults.

The Reformers insisted that all persons are sinners, from their conception.[5] Sin is not only acts but a continual inclination of our nature that permeates all that we do, even those acts that appear to be good.[6] Sin is therefore no mere external impediment but a deep corruption of the entire human nature.[7] This inborn or original sin is a matter of personal responsibility and is truly sin, condemning to God's wrath all who are not born again through Baptism and the Holy Spirit.[8] Such original sin involves not only bodily desires but carnal wisdom and righteousness; it involves ignorance and contempt of God; lack of fear and trust in God, and inability to love God.[9] Being a sinner for the Reformers meant more than not having true faith in God; it meant being unable to do so by nature. Even though fallen human beings cannot but sin, the Reformers held that this sin is culpable; humanity is guilty and hence under the wrath of God.

Human beings are both creatures of God and sinners at the same time—creatures, that is, who have lost the image of God, who have lost the wisdom and righteousness that grasps and reflects God, that fears and trusts him.[10] This loss or "fall" is the direct responsibility of humankind and not something for which we can blame God. The Reformers held that it was important to distinguish between human nature as created good by God and the sinful disposition which we have which is not to be attributed to God.[11]

Paul Tillich, whose method has already proven useful for our purpose, has some helpful insights on the matter of interpreting "sin" for students today. He points out that in the 20th century the word *sin* has predominantly and wrongly been used in the plural ("sins" as deviations from moral laws). Your students may very likely be most familiar with this usage. The problem, then, is to help students appreciate the depth of sin as an ongoing state, not merely an occasional act that we commit—that is, to help the students understand sin as an ongoing inclination or corruption in our nature. Tillich suggests that the term *estrangement* is often helpful in pointing to that predicament in which we are not what we essentially are and ought to be. He speaks of estrangement from that to which one essentially belongs—that is, from God, from one's self, and from one's world.[12]

Tillich believed that the term *estrangement* was a useful one since the work of Freud and psychoanalysis as well as literature enabled persons in this century to understand the concept of estrangement in a way that is helpful for understanding the basic human predicament. Now, although times have changed since Tillich wrote, there is a sense in which what he suggested may be even truer today. Our experiences of estrangement have taken new forms in our increasingly pluralistic society even while the influence and language of psychology has become yet more widely pervasive than when he wrote. Sadly, few children or teenagers or adults in our society do not know the tragedy of estrangement either in their own family or in that of friends, relatives, or acquaintances. The increase in divorce in the last two decades has brought home vividly the tragedy of estrangement between persons. Racial tension, international tension and wars, terrorism, sexism, violence in homes and on the streets, the arms race, are as vivid testimony in our own times of estrangement in our predicament as the ancient biblical accounts of hostility against God, other individuals, other nations, and against oneself. Estrangement from others is a deeply experienced *question* in our society. What may be more difficult for contemporary persons to grasp is the concept of estrangement from God. Many liberation theologians write as if the primary component in sin is a horizontal one—oppression between persons and structures in society and the world. In teaching we shall need to preserve both the horizontal and the vertical dimension, the truth that we are estranged from others but also from God and from ourselves. In fact, the estrangement from God lies at the heart of estrangement from others and from ourselves.

However, in addition, Tillich held that the term *sin* must be retained because it carries with it the added connotation of the personal act of turning away from that to which one belongs. That is, it points to personal responsibility for estrangement. While all humankind is involved in the predicament, nevertheless we cannot escape our own personal freedom and guilt in the matter.[13] As individuals we turn toward ourselves and our world and away from God in knowledge, will, and emotions. Or, another way to put it, is that we love self and the world for their own sake and fail to see beyond them to the God who brought both into being and who is Lord of both.[14] Or yet again, sin is complete self-centeredness and the elevation of ourselves to the sphere of the divine, making ourselves to be like God, making ourselves the center of the universe. The wonderfully insightful story in Genesis 3 gets at the heart of temptation in verse 5—"and you will be like God." That is what we want to be! Martin Luther understood that to make ourselves the center of the world, to be like God, is the "greatest idolatry"; he knew that the whole point of works righteousness is setting ourselves up as God's lords, "setting up ourselves as God" and so making God into an idol.[15]

In teaching, then, you may want to use the term *estrangement*. But you will also want to use the word *sin* as an irreplaceable item of theological vocabulary. Sometimes you may want to use terms such as *hostility* toward or *alienation* from God, others, and self. The important thing is to help your students define the terms and to fill them with good theological content. Use stories and biblical illustrations as well as illustrations from your students' own lives to enrich meaning. Then label the illustrations with the appropriate terminology.

As a check-list in teaching students, consider the following points on the "human question."

Sin is
- elevating ourselves to the place of God
- self-centeredness
- estrangement from God, others, self
- ignorance and contempt of, hostility toward God
- lack of trust in God

Sin is
- universal (except for Jesus)
- affects all human beings from conception
- the responsibility of human beings, not God
- an inclination and deep corruption of our whole nature
- also the acts that result from that inclination
- to be taken very seriously
- something that involves us totally—knowledge, will, emotions, and actions

And we
- bear personal responsibility for sin
- are guilty
- deserve God's wrath and judgment
- are unable not to sin
- are creatures of God as well as sinners
- are sinners and also saved simultaneously

Of course, you will not use all of these concepts with younger age levels. In succeeding chapters we shall consider those points most appropriately used with children and youth, and how to "translate" them for maximum comprehension. However, even when a point is not suitable for an age-level, be sure that you do not inadvertently teach the opposite. For example, with children you will not want to overemphasize God's wrath and judgment. But avoid the opposite extreme of implying that God does not really care about sin at all. By carefully selecting what you will say, you can avoid giving the wrong impression. In this way teachers of youth and adults will be able to build on the excellent foundation you have laid.

The answer

We saw that justification by grace through faith was considered by the 16th-century Reformers to be the main doctrine of Christianity. Confessional documents emphasize that justification is solely a matter of God's grace, never our own works. We can do nothing to make ourselves right with God or to rid ourselves of sin. We can never earn God's favor or forgiveness by doing good deeds. Justification is entirely the work of God and is due solely to his love and mercy. It is the forgiveness of sins, reconciliation, the acceptance of the sinner by God in spite of his or her sinfulness.

The reconciliation of humanity to God is due to the work of Christ, not to works of the law. Salvation is due to the merits of Christ alone. Only Christ in his obedience and suffering provides the means for our forgiveness. The reformers emphasized the cross and suffering of Christ as obedience in perfectly keeping God's law so that God reckons his righteousness to us and forgives our sins.[16] God imputes, declares righteous, esteems righteous, pronounces us righteous, for the sake of Christ. And this righteousness is appropriated and accepted by faith.[17] Faith itself is a gift of God. The gift of faith enables us to know Christ as Savior and to trust in him for forgiveness of sin by grace, and thus faith is acceptance of the merits of Christ.[18]

Good works are not a means to earn God's mercy. But our response of thanks and trust for God's forgiveness issues joyfully in good works that serve our neighbor. Works, then, are a response to God's love and forgiveness, not a means of obtaining them.

Such traditional phrases may sound familiar to many of your students who will have sung them in hymns and read them in Scripture. But familiarity does not necessarily mean that understanding is present. The terms are not those that one might find on the lips of adults in the street, let alone in the mouths of adolescents or children. Like *sin,* these terms need interpretation and explanation.

Tillich believed that a helpful way to get at the *answer* in this century was to focus on Paul's message of the new creation in Christ—or, the message of the "New Being." Such a message Tillich insists must include reconciliation and forgiveness of sins which were the concerns of the Reformers. But it "centers around what we might call 'healing reality,' around the courage to say 'yes' in the encounter with nothingness, anxiety, and despair." [19] Another way he put it was to say that the estrangement between ourselves and God, ourselves and others, and ourselves and ourselves is overcome. [20]

Tillich suggested that the legal imagery of justification is not the best way to communicate justification in the mid-to-late 20th century. He used instead the term *acceptance*. It was no doubt fortuitous that psychoanalysis had popularized the notion of acceptance by the time he wrote. People thus had a new tool that helped them ask the question to which the gospel answer could be correlated. People were more able to express anxiety about the meaning of existence, including problems of faith, death, and guilt. In the past couple of decades psychological categories have continued to pervade our society and culture. Those who do counseling will bear testimony to the expression of such anxiety. Therefore, the term *acceptance* continues to be a helpful one to use in teaching about God's justification. But, it is most important that if we use the term *acceptance*—and it does indeed work well in teaching children as well as youth and adults—that we follow Tillich's lead in filling the term with the meaning of the Reformation understanding of justification. In other words, the important point is not the term (which is merely a tool to aid communication) but the theological content that is given to the term. As a matter of fact, 16th century confessional documents use the term *acceptance* as a synonym for justification and forgiveness of sins. [21] To borrow a term that has been widely used in our century, but to fill it with the fullness of the biblical understanding of God's merciful forgiveness of the sinner, is a helpful device in teaching because the hearer is more likely to listen and grasp what the message is all about. But the technique can, however, have a drawback if the hearer hears only a partial definition of acceptance—for example, if the hearer were to understand a weak tolerance on God's part for the sinner, as if God "puts up with" or perhaps, does not even notice, sin. This would be to misuse the term. It is most important that the central "in spite of" be retained—the miracle that God accepts the sinner *in spite of* the fact that she or he is unacceptable! Now, that is miraculous grace!

In the classroom we can also follow Tillich in using examples from life to point beyond themselves to the unconditional acceptance which human beings need. For example, Tillich sees in the healing process in our world, a fragmentary healing—actually a part of the *question* that points to the need for real healing. But real healing, perfect healing, can only come through new creation, being made whole through Jesus. A patient's need in psychoanalysis for acceptance from another, and the impossibility of self-acceptance without such a prior acceptance from another, point to our need for ultimate acceptance that can only come from God. God's acceptance is the only acceptance that truly fills our deepest need and that can genuinely issue in self-acceptance and so in acceptance of others. In this sense, Tillich would use psychoanalytic case-studies as instances of the question, calling for the answer, pointing toward the answer, but not themselves being part of the answer.[22] The answer can only come from God's revelation. Only a gospel that contradicts our experience, that comes from outside of our experience, can provide the answer we need.[23]

You can use experiences of acceptance in families, peer groups, the church, and in your own class to point toward God's acceptance. Of course, all of the acceptance which your students will have experienced in this world, no matter how apparently self-less, has some element of condition about it. But God's acceptance has no conditions. It is pure gift and pure grace. So experiences in the lives of students can be no more than pointers toward God's good news.

Forgiveness and *reconciliation* are also terms that mean much today and can be used extensively. The acceptance of the prodigal son by his father can be a powerful image of reconciliation in today's society that is riddled with family difficulties, separation, divorce, runaway teenagers, and other experiences of division.

Youth and adults often have deep doubt in today's secular society. Tillich believed that a danger in our century is the legalism that insists on belief in some particular religious tenet about God and the legalism that eschews doubt of any kind. Such legalism is just as much of a burden as legalism in morals. The doctrine of justification breaks through all legalism. Just at the very moment when we are most aware that we do not have exactly the right words, or even when we have radical doubt, just at the moment when we are most aware that we have no good works that can help us deal with our sinfulness; then in that moment we may hear the word of the gospel assuring us that God has broken the power of legalism and accepts us in spite of our doubts and our hostility.[24]

In a world in which meaninglessness and radical doubt threaten along with annihilation of the whole human race, we must present God as answer to that meaninglessness and the one who is Lord of the universe. We can affirm that the source of forgiveness and healing and of hope lies in God, not in humanity.

A summary may be of help in listing the points to keep in mind when communicating justification.

Justification is

- forgiveness of sin
- reconciliation or healing of the estrangement between ourselves and God
- acceptance of the sinner by God *in spite of* guilt, estrangement, hostility, self-centeredness
- being set in a right relationship with God
- new life, new creation, "New Being"

Justification is

- due to God's grace, God's unconditional and undeserved love
- a free gift of God

- not the result of anything we *do*
- not the result of the law
- being treated *as if* we were righteous even though we are not
- being declared righteous for Christ's sake
- due to the merits of Christ alone
- due to Christ's obedience and suffering
- not a glib overlooking of sin but a serious and costly dealing with sin
- something we need daily since, though saved, we also continue to sin
- accepted by faith which is itself a gift of God
- available for all who trust in God for forgiveness
- that which gives us hope for the future and the courage to say yes in the face of meaninglessness and despair

Justification results in
- joyous thanksgiving to God
- a response of love and good works in service to others
- sharing the good news with others
- sharing in suffering and the way of the cross

Christ the answer

Someone may say, But isn't Christ himself the answer to the human question? And the answer, of course, is yes! Often, when we teach about Christ, we ask students to grasp exceedingly difficult and technical information about Christ's person. Making a distinction between Christ's person and work has a long tradition in Christian theology. However, there is a sense in which the two are inevitably intertwined. Sixteenth-century Reformers held that merely knowing about the immanent Trinity is not really knowing God, and that knowing about the person of Christ in two natures is not to know Christ. Melanchthon's statement that to know Christ is to know his benefits is a fundamental principle of the Lutheran Confessions, and "to know the benefits of Christ is to receive these benefits; it is the reality of the act of the incarnate Son of God for me and upon me."[25]

Martin Luther held that the second article of the Creed can be summarized in the word *Lord* as Redeemer and that the remaining parts of the article simply express how and by what means redemption was accomplished.[26] For the Reformers, the important focus was trust that the incarnate Son of God has redeemed, delivered, and freed me from all sins.[27] Because Christ was truly God, his obedience can be reckoned to us as righteousness; and because Christ was truly human his righteousness is reckoned as our righteousness.[28] Christ's divine and human natures are necessary in order to achieve salvation. The exalted Christ continues to dwell in the church as truly God and truly human, coming to us in the Lord's Supper which is a proclamation of the forgiveness of sins.[29]

This soteriological focus will be helpful in teaching. Speaking of two natures is often difficult for adults to comprehend, let alone adolescents. (And children would think literally of two persons inhabiting the same body—a sort of multiple personality!) But, if we bear in mind that the point of Christology is the assurance of our salvation then we may place our emphasis on that point. Salvation in fact is manifested in Jesus in whom we see sinless humanity in perfect relationship with God—the very expression of what we human beings were intended to be and are not.

Faith

We use the term *acceptance* in two ways. Justification is understood as God's gracious acceptance of the sinner in spite of guilt. And faith is understood as acceptance of the promise of the gospel.[30] Justification is the act in which God accepts us in spite of our guilt, estrangement, hostility, and self-centeredness. And, in spite of our anxiety, we accept through faith that gracious acceptance of us by God.[31]

Faith is centrally related to Christ. It is the certainty that Christ is the center of our history and that he has won the victory over estrangement. And it has this certainty because it is based on an experience of being grasped by the power of Christ through whom the consequences of sin are conquered.[32]

Our faith is not some kind of work that can earn God's favor. Instead, it is a gift from God by which to receive the free gift of forgiveness of sin. God grasps us in the totality of our being and gives us a total response of trust. Since this is God's own action, it is a matter of grace.

It is the Word that calls us to faith—and proclamation of the Word is precisely what you are about in teaching the gospel. So you may pray expectantly for the miracle of faith in your students.

Faith is a whole-person response, a centering of one's life. We said in Chapter 1 that faith is partly volitional, partly emotive, and partly cognitive. As teachers we must take seriously the cognitive and the emotional and the volitional aspects of our students. And we cannot equate faith with any one of the three: it is never purely a matter of will, nor purely of emotion, nor purely of cognition. Rather, faith is an act of the whole person, a centered act of personal commitment. Therefore, our goals should reflect this holistic viewpoint. Lesson objectives should not imply that the gospel can be reduced to a set of beliefs that can be learned by rote, nor simply a set of feelings to exhibit, nor just an act of will to be expressed in specific ways. Objectives should be worded in ways that help us present the good news of God's acceptance of the whole student and that encourage a whole-person response of trust in God's mercy.

Any communication of knowledge in religious education must be existential knowledge—knowledge that affects my existence radically. We will not be looking for purely intellectual assent to information, but rather seeking engagement with the message that grasps the very center of the students' existence.

> To communicate the gospel means putting it before the people so that they are able to decide for or against it. The Christian gospel is a matter of decision. It is to be accepted or rejected. All that we who communicate this gospel can do is to make possible a genuine decision. Such a decision is one based on understanding and on partial participation.[33]

There is a role of conceptuality in religious education, of course. Tillich says that "the great art of the religious educator is to transform the primitive literalism with respect to the religious symbols into a conceptual interpretation without destroying the power of the symbols."[34] But, we shall not be interested in merely showing that the students can reflect cognitively about the gospel. We shall want the students to appropriate the good news and receive it as that which affects their lives.

Of course, in teaching it will always be easier to evaluate the cognitive dimension of the communication rather than the affective or volitional. And ultimately, the faith response is something that only God can know, although there will be behavioral pointers that may be considered consistent with a response of faith. But we must resist the temptation to limit educational goals to the purely cognitive element.

In addition to holistic objectives, it will be important to have a mixture of procedures in class sessions so that neither cognition nor feelings nor will are overemphasized but all are treated about equally. Cognitive reasoning must be balanced with decision to commitment and action and also with affective and creative activities. Using imagination, expressing feelings, developing and experiencing attitudes, praising and worshiping, are as important as studying creedal statements and discussing understandings and viewpoints. (We shall say more about creative imaginative activities in Chapter 8.)

The view of faith presented here is somewhat different from that used by some contemporary researchers. Despite James Fowler's contention that his view of faith reflects that of Tillich,[35] it can be argued that his view is decidedly different. First, Fowler assumes that all persons have faith; he does not distinguish between that trust which is idolatrous and that which has the true God as its focus. Second, Fowler develops his understanding of faith with a decided cognitive bias. Now, this is probably not his intention. As a structuralist, Fowler wants to suggest that the structures exhibited in faith will organize the whole of a person's emotions and social relationships,[36] and claims that his six stages of faith cannot be reduced to cognitive or moral stages.[37] However, in practice, Fowler's theory of faith-stages comes across as highly cognitive, falling into the trap of holding that there is a qualitative increase in adequacy in each stage of faith development[38] and that the movement through the first three stages at least depends on cognitive development.

Faith as whole-person commitment or trust or utter dependence that is a gift of the Spirit cannot be measured in "stages" nor is it quantifiable in any way.[39] Fowler's view of spiraling faith misses this essential gift-quality of faith. And probably must do so, to avoid some theologically embarrassing conclusions—one could hardly defend the notion that God gives the gracious gift of faith less adequately to children than to adults, and does so on the basis of their cognitive development until the early teens and then on the basis of their social and affective experiences! Nor the corollary that salvation would then depend upon cognitive development and social-emotional experiences! The difference between Tillich and Fowler is the essential soteriological concern of the former. For Tillich it is salvation that is uppermost in his discussion of faith. Faith is the response to God's promise, the means of appropriating the gospel. It is the acceptance of God's prior acceptance of us despite our sinfulness. If faith were to be separated from justification, then it perhaps could be a purely interesting sociological phenomenon that could be researched. But, if salvation is at stake, then any quantitative or qualitative variations in faith must be repudiated. For God in his grace gives his gift totally and equally to all in order that his gracious forgiveness may be received fully. God does not partially justify or justify to a less or more adequate extent some rather than others. It is important that teachers of children particularly grasp this fact. Sometimes teachers are inclined to think that the work with children isn't quite in the same category as the "real" teaching of the gospel to youth and adults. But the faith of a child is also the gift of God and is very precious. To teach the gospel to young learners is an important undertaking. Every human being from the youngest to the oldest is in need of God's good news. The human question is as real and painful for the child as for the adult. And God's answer is as relevant and comforting to the child as to the older student.

Ronald Goldman's thesis that children are prereligious and then subreligious until adolescence is open to some of the same objections as Fowler's. Goldman is clear that his task is researching solely the cognitive understanding of religious concepts and he acknowledges that religion cannot be reduced to an intellectual exercise. However, his goal for teachers is that some of the students will reach the point where they can embrace Christian beliefs either as they leave school (about age 17) or later in adulthood.[40] Goldman's concern not to overload children with conceptual material that is beyond them is laudable. But it seems that for Goldman an overly-large component of faith is the grasp of intellectually-appropriate concepts. In overemphasizing the cognitive, the religious educator runs the risk of distorting faith and perhaps of failing to seek new ways to help children hear the gospel. If children really participate in the human predicament and need the answer of the gospel, then we must attempt to find ways of helping them hear that answer which is good news for them too.

Now, if we seek to engage students in their affective as well as cognitive and volitional dimensions, then we may also expect that as teachers we shall be wholly involved in the teaching task. Any communication of the message of justification can never be casually "passing on information." To teach the gospel is directly to challenge our students' existence at its very root. This means that teaching the gospel will sometimes be an emotionally taxing experience for both you and your students. Not that you will deliberately seek to infuse the situation with false emotion. That would do a disservice to the gospel. But the fact is that the gospel deals with the very depths of our human existence, challenging all of our self-deception and self-love, stripping away our trust in ourselves and our ability to save ourselves, revealing us as naked and guilty. Little surprise that emotion will be involved when faced with the genuine question and the incredible answer of a gracious God who accepts us "in spite of" what we are.

Symbols in teaching

In teaching, we shall be using the symbolic power of language constantly. Language about God takes symbols from daily experience and applies them to the One who is beyond our finite experience.[41] The language of symbol and myth is the language of faith.[42] We can't speak of God any other way simply because we are finite creatures and can speak of God only indirectly. Now, Tillich uses the term *symbol* in a very rich way. For him, a symbol actually participates in that to which it points. First, it participates in the honor appropriate to that which it represents (for example, consider the honor that we accord to the flag which represents our nation), and second, it participates in the power of that which it represents (for example, a New Testament story about Jesus can actually mediate to us the power of the original event which it describes).[43] A biblical story about someone else may not only show us what others are like; it may actually give us a picture of our own selves and of God's action for us. In this sense, it becomes a means of salvation.

In the classroom, we shall constantly be seeking the symbols which will make most sense to our students. Some symbols mean more to one age-level than another. Some mean more in one era than another. As we seek for the most appropriate symbols to use with our students, we must bear in mind Tillich's warning that symbols can be demonic as well as divine. A demonic symbol is one that points towards itself. Another way to put it would be to say that it gets in the way of the message; it is destructive. A divine symbol is one that truly mediates the power of God to the learner and is healing.[44] Now, all symbols are limited to the finite. They point beyond themselves, and yet they participate in our worldly reality. There is always the possibility that the learner will not grasp that to which they point. We are to seek those symbols that will communicate as clearly as possible to our students, so they may stake their lives upon the One to whom the symbolic language points.

Chapter 4

GOOD NEWS
FOR CHILDREN

In Chapter 1 we mentioned the difficulty of communicating the gospel to children. Some researchers would argue that, since the child cannot comprehend cognitively either "sin" or "justification," then we should not attempt to teach these matters until the age of formal operations. For the person genuinely to grasp what sin is and to appropriate salvation, these researchers would argue that the child must have the cognitive maturity to make sense of these realities. Even if presented in story form, the meaning is "trapped" for people until they are about 12 years of age[1]; the meaning cannot be grasped cognitively. Should we then simply omit the teaching of God's merciful forgiveness of sinful human beings until the teenage years, when the brain cells are sufficiently mature for the child to appreciate cognitively the human situation and God's activity in dealing with that situation?

The serious problem with this suggestion is that, by delaying teaching until the young adolescent is cognitively ready to comprehend the Christian faith, children are necessarily prevented from hearing the gospel in a meaningful way that relates to their existential situation. Now, this might make sense if we were to assume that the child does not need the gospel—that is, if we were to hold that the child is not a sinner. But, we have already said that all members of the human race without exception are in fact sinners from the moment of conception. So, all children are sinful human beings for whom the human *question* is a reality.

In this case, not to teach children of God's *answer* would mean that they would be left with no answer to their human predicament. Or else it might assume that children live in blissful ignorance of any particular need of God and of his love and that both the need and the gospel can be brought to consciousness at adolescence. To dispel this notion, we shall give evidence below that the child is aware of deep needs (some on a conscious level, and some at deeper levels of the personality) to which the answer of the gospel is not only relevant but indeed imperative. In fact, failing to teach the gospel is to fail to deal with the child's very deepest needs.

Must we then revert to teaching children as miniature adults and thus ignore their cognitive development altogether? But cognitive research is descriptive of God's own creation. We cannot ignore that creation—or imply that God made a mistake in permitting persons to develop in a slow stage-pattern. We are constantly learning more about human development and thus about the wonderful way in which God's creation is manifest in humanity. Cognitive research must be taken account of and respected, and church leaders and teachers need constantly to keep abreast of findings that add to our information about our students. This means that we cannot teach the cognitive component of the gospel message to children in exactly the same way that we do to adults. But at the same time, we cannot give up communicating to children the good news of God's gracious forgiveness. So, we must first recognize our young students' need of the gospel and then seek ways of communicating both an expression of the need (to help the children focus those experiences which they already have) and of the gospel message so that God and his love are seen as relevant by the children to their own situation. Such means of communication must be chosen carefully to fit the ways in which children think and perceive meaning. They must also take account of the understanding of the gospel as encompassing more than the merely cognitive component; communication of the gospel must be that which engages the whole child in a response of trust and commitment to the One who justifies by grace.

The appropriate question for us to ask is, Are there ways of communicating the gospel to children that do not violate the child's development and that also maintain theological integrity? Our answer is that there may be a number of such tools waiting to be discovered. In Chapter 5 we shall describe just one which has already been used with success with children. It is the tool of transformationally-structured narrative (narrative structured according to a particular five-step pattern). This tool has been shown useful with children ages eight to eleven.[2] It is possible that transformational narrative could be used in education with children younger than eight years; even five-year-olds respond therapeutically to such structured narrative. But at this stage more research needs to be done to determine the value of this tool in teaching younger children. However, the eight-to-eleven-year span may be an excellent level to focus on. On the face of it, justification is one of the least likely doctrines to be able to be communicated to a child in the concrete thinking stage. The concrete-thinking child is typically law-oriented and preoccupied with works or earning favor fairly. Grace appears to be directly opposed to the developmental stage of the concrete thinker. It could be said that the child just does not seem to be ready to hear of a gracious God who deals with persons in ways other than law and works.[3] It is, therefore, a challenge to take the law-oriented child and to attempt to communicate grace in a way that is comprehended and seen as relevant by the child.

Children and the "question"

Do children have any real experience of the *question* or are they in blissful ignorance? Even common sense would suggest that children experience estrangement deeply in their own lives and those of others. Psychologists can help us elucidate such

56

experiences. By starting with children's experiences that cry out for God's *answer*, we can relate the gospel to those experiences and so avoid "throwing the gospel like a stone" at the children.[4] The gospel should be that which children recognize as eminently relevant to their lives.

From birth the child experiences deep alienation, disruption, and estrangement. Freud pointed out that from early childhood an individual exhibits self-centeredness, negation, estrangement from reality, hostility, aggression, guilt, and cruelty.[5] While due to repression, the aggression, destructiveness, guilt, hostility, and estrangement from reality are often unconscious, these factors continue to be part of the child's development. By middle child-hood the person has learned many acceptable behaviors by which to avoid showing these traits too often to family and peers. How-ever, these characteristics are inevitably present in the child and split the child from himself and others. Not all such experiences are readily available to the child consciously nor can the child necessarily express all of them. But this does not mean that they are not real. Nor does it mean that they are not painful and in need of answers.

Richard Gardiner notes that research in children's fantasy stories shows that violence and aggression are the dominant themes.[6] Hostility and anger particularly are shown. Such aggres-sion and hostility are typical of all children, not merely those with pathological morbidity. Thus we can expect that children will readily be able to handle the *question* side of the correlation in terms of hostility and aggression. The *answer* of grace and forgiveness in spite of what we are like or what we have done is the antithesis of this "dominant theme" and is decidedly an an-swer from "outside" of the child.[7]

Of course, psychologists such as Freud and Gardiner can only point to instances of separation of the child from herself or himself and others. The biblical writers know that the child also stands guilty before God as one who has "fallen" from that which humanity was created to be. And although this predicament is common to all developing human beings, each child is involved personally and responsibly in the hostility and estrangement from reality, from herself, from others, and from God. Psychoanalytic healing can help with misplaced or neurotic guilt but is no solution to correctly-placed guilt, from the estrangement that is at the heart of the human problem for persons of all ages.[8] The answer to the child's existential estrangement must come from outside of our human situation, from the God who speaks a Word of unconditional acceptance in Jesus the Christ.[9]

Children also have experiences of acceptance that call for and point to the *answer* of God's acceptance. In middle childhood, for example, the family, school, and peer relationships provide ambiguous experiences of conditional acceptance that can be used in teaching to point to the answer, although they are themselves not the answer. Social psychologists give us many instances of this ambiguous and inadequate prototype of acceptance—experiences that are very important for the elementary child and show a deep need for unconditional acceptance. You can take these experiences into account in communicating the message of justification to elementary-age children. They are most likely to be the concrete instances to which the children will refer in classroom discussion and which they will use to make sense of the meaning of *acceptance*. It will be important to affirm their experiences of acceptance and yet also to help the children realize that such experiences are never experiences of unconditional acceptance and that the acceptance we need is ultimately to be found only in God.

The family is the main base of security and identity during most of the elementary years.[10] Elementary children want to be accepted into their parents' confidence and their "secret" discussions.[11] Children may interpret overly strict or overly lenient behavior as parental rejection and lack of acceptance.[12] They demand that parents give evidence of their commitment in terms of time and interest devoted to the children's endeavors.[13] Need for parental acceptance is so important that a child with deep-seated feelings of hostility or aggression is more likely to express the hostility toward peers or toward himself than to express it openly and directly against the parents.[14] Parental acceptance is closely related to the way in which children view themselves; a child who feels loved and accepted tends to see herself that way and so her self-esteem is high.[15]

However, while the child has deep needs for parental acceptance, there is no experience of this acceptance that is not ambiguously mixed with alienation, guilt, estrangement, and hostility. Parental pressure to succeed results in the child's experiences of failure in the family, in experiences of rejection, of being not-accepted. Acceptance in the family can never be more than partial since even the best of parents are part of the human race with its self-centeredness and estrangement from God. Even in the most accepting family, the child experiences rejection, alienation, and estrangement between himself and his family members. The acceptance of parents is in fact no more nor less than prototype—a pale foretaste and hint of the acceptance that the child needs in her deepest self. The child needs an Other who can accept, heal, and forgive; who can genuinely overcome estrangement and bring wholeness; a self-affirming Other who can answer the child's deepest needs. This Other must come from outside the family because parental acceptance can be always only a broken indication of the acceptance which the child needs. In this sense the family is a part of the human *question,* pointing only to the shape of the *answer.* The God who will be good news for the child may well reflect the qualities of a perfect, accepting parent.

A second major factor in the lives of elementary children is that of school. Teacher acceptance is an important factor in the child's development. It is correlated with peer acceptance of students[16] and also with students' own perception of themselves.[17] As in the family, acceptance by this significant adult is no more and no less than a prototype of the acceptance that the child seeks at her deepest level. Elementary teachers are important persons in the lives of their students. By their acceptance of their students—even in spite of students' unacceptableness!—their classroom relationships can give the children opportunity to experience human acceptance as prototype of the divine acceptance. Yet teacher acceptance will be as ambiguous and as conditional as any other human acceptance, an experience of the *question,* although also an analog of the *answer* of the gospel.

The child's peers become increasingly important during the elementary years until, in adolescence, the self becomes embedded in mutuality and interpersonal relationships.[18] Acceptance by the peer group is very important for children and they fear rejection by their age-mates.[19] As with parent and teacher acceptance, peer acceptance influences the child's self-acceptance.[20] And again, peer acceptance can be no ultimate answer to the child's need for unconditional acceptance. Peers are part of the very situation of estrangement, part of the *question* side of the correlation. Yet, peer acceptance also may act as prototype, pointing toward the kind of acceptance which the child needs that can only be received from God.

As the child proceeds through the elementary years, the concept of "fair" develops. The concrete operational child is a legalist. Right is seen as that which is fair, and each person deserves to be praised or punished according to the rightness or wrongness of an action. Thus, when children transgress the mores or values or rules of family, school, or peers, they usually consider it fair that they should be rejected. So the concrete operational child faces again and again the unpleasant dilemma of acknowledging the "fairness" of rejection while crying out inwardly for acceptance. The child, in other words, judges herself worthy of rejection but longs for unconditional and unbroken acceptance. Theologically, we would say that the child stands under the law and in need of grace. The needs of the child might thus be expressed in two ways—"Who accepts me as I am?" and "Who accepts me when parents and teachers and friends reject me— and even when I think that I deserve to be rejected?" The child longs for healing, wholeness, self-affirmation, and unconditional acceptance. Only God's acceptance in Christ can fulfill the child's deepest needs. Only God can provide the acceptance which the estranged child seeks in his or her daily relationships.

Other aspects of sin that are particularly relevant to the con-crete-thinking child are conflict, hostility, wanting to go one's own way, loneliness, and destructive suffering. Stories that deal with conflict and hostility between persons and their families or their peers or important authority figures portray situations which children can readily recognize. Also appropriate are narratives that deal with personal responsibility and guilt in children's terms and those which deal with self-centeredness. Helpful too will be stories that deal with the despair of making things right by one's own efforts or natural processes and which look for Another outside of oneself and the developmental process who can trans-form and make life new. Narrative and discussion should reflect the longings which are part of the elementary years—the yearning for inclusiveness yet distinctiveness, for dependence yet inde-pendence, for a loving other in the face of loneliness, for self-affirmation which depends on God's affirmation, forgiveness, and reintegration of the divided self.

Estrangement in the developmental process

Some thinkers point to estrangement as part of the actual developmental process. Robert Kegan speaks of the self as an "evolving self." The child moves through a succession of stages of development, each with particular intellectual, social, emo-tional, and physical characteristics. During any given stage, the child has no choice but to totally be immersed or embedded in that stage.[21] Growth involves the emergence from embeddedness so that the child takes as object that to which she was previously subject. Moving into a new stage involves a new subjectivity from which the child will later emerge as transition is made to yet the next stage. In every stage of development there is am-bivalence in the person—a yearning to be included and a yearning to be autonomous, to be dependent and also to be independent, a desire for integration and a desire for differentiation. The self moves back and forth between a resolution of this ambivalent tension in favor of one side at one stage and the other at the next.

The young child—the impulsive self—tends to be overintegrated. The imperial self of the concrete operational stage is overdifferentiated and has a strong focus on the self. The interpersonal self of the early teenager shows the overintegrated character again and focuses on others.[22]

In the transition from one stage to another, Kegan believes that the self faces the threat of non-being. Emerging from the previous stage, the self senses its own inadequacy and may confront its own sinfulness, disloyalty, idolatry.[23] The self senses that its organization is not working.[24] The self recognizes that there is something deeply wrong with her or him and in this threat to self-affirmation faces non-being. Moving from one "self" to the next, the person experiences being self and not-self simultaneously.[25] Regular development thus has within it a sort of experience of estrangement—a separation of self, an experience of non-being. Any child, according to Kegan, knows something of the meaning of the threat of non-being, the loss of the self, some experience of estrangement which Kegan links to that of Tillich.[26] This developmental estrangement is by no means the full depth of theological or existential estrangement. In fact, it belongs to what Tillich would call the area of preliminary concerns. Existential estrangement is an ongoing matter throughout all of life, not merely in periods of transition between developmental stages. And existential estrangement involves more than an experience of non-being of the previous self that one has been in an evolutionary truce. It is rather radical estrangement from God and includes personal guilt and turning away from God and thus from the courage to be in spite of non-being. Nevertheless, from Kegan we learn that the children in our classes will already have some experience of estrangement, that the notion will not be unfamiliar to them.

We have seen that the human question involves self-centeredness. Kegan's thesis is that the concrete-thinking child or the imperial self shows an imbalance in favor of overdifferentiation, that is, the child is self-centered. The imperial self typically shows the overdifferentiated issues of self-esteem, competence, self-display, and personal aggrandizement.[27] He or she is embedded in his or her own needs and wishes. This self-centeredness suggests that in the presentation of the question with elementary students you may well emphasize the understanding of sin as making oneself the center of one's world and the focus of all reality.[28] The self-centeredness of the imperial child does not mean that elementary children are more sinful than other human beings. But it does mean that in raising the question with children, the teacher will appropriately raise the issue of sin as self-centeredness which is an important aspect of the children's developmental experience. In fact, the self-centeredness of the imperial self is a reminder of the self-centeredness of all of us that calls for a recentering of the person by the gracious action of a powerful and gracious Other who accepts and forgives the self which is not what it ought to be.

Kegan believes that, in the transitions between stages, the person not only faces non-being in giving up the old self on behalf of a possible new self, but the self also finds the courage to be precisely between the prior self-affirmation and the future self-affirmation.[29] Thus Kegan believes that in the developmental process itself is the answer to the threat of non-being. He basically views the process positively as descriptive of hope.[30] But we are less optimistic than Kegan about deriving the answer from the developmental process. In fact, the process of individualization and participation itself participates in the ambiguities of estrangement under the conditions of existence. The self-integrative process is ambiguously mixed with disintegration in every life process, not merely in evolutionary truces.[31] The estrangement of sin is experienced at every moment in life, including the transitions between stages. The *answer* must come from outside of the developmental process, from the Creator of all developmental processes, who is beyond the process and who includes both individualization and participation and transcends them both.[32]

An understanding of the depth of sin and guilt calls for a much more radical answer than does the lesser problem which

Kegan addresses of simply recognizing a stage embeddedness as being inadequate to cope with life's experiences. But, Kegan's analysis of the developmental process with its successive imbalances points up the human *question* sharply. Imbalance after imbalance, the ego tries to correct the situation and is unable to do so. The imbalance shows evidence of the continuous struggle with disintegration; it is a distortion of what the person ought to be. The developmental process calls for an answer it cannot give. It is, in other words, very much a part of the human *question*. Only a power beyond the child can deal with the alienation and estrangement which are at the root of the individualization-participation process as it is experienced in human existence. Only the answer of God's intervention in Jesus Christ is adequate to bring healing to divided, separated existence. The only self which has true unity is the person who knows that he or she is accepted as a unity in spite of his or her disunity.[33] Such acceptance involves a gift-quality; it is a matter of grace.

Like Kegan, James Loder also sees the question of human existence in stage transitions. Loder analyzes the developmental transition process to show that it is governed by the pattern of transformational logic which we shall examine in Chapter 5.[34] But, unlike Kegan, Loder does not find the answer within the process itself. The developmental answer he sees as prototype of the real answer that is needed. But that real answer lies outside of the process itself. Stage transitional transformation needs transformation through encounter with Christ; in the divine transformation of transformation lies the answer to the human question.

Points to keep in mind when teaching

Even young children may well express the notion of estrangement, although obviously they will not use that word to describe it. But preoperational children (in the thinking stage from about two to seven years) are not capable of logical reasoning and often feel guilty about things which adults would consider are not their fault. Therefore, it will be very important not to overteach the *question*. It must be their experience of the question to which we listen, not our own adult experience that we thrust upon the child. Only too often young children already live in a world of constant do's, don'ts, and guilt. In many ways the very young need more gospel than law. Until we know God's merciful love, the law cannot drive us to that mercy. So young children particularly need to hear good news.

During the concrete-thinking stage, children grow in ability to deal with classes and generalizations.[35] They still find easiest the manner of thinking that typifies the preoperational stage from which they have emerged, in which the child thinks of discrete items and acts, rather than classes. Therefore children will most likely readily identify sin in terms of individual acts. In other words, elementary children will tend to comprehend sin in the very way in which Tillich reacts against the use of the term—that is, in the "plural" sense of "sins" or specific instances of words, thoughts, and deeds, which the children have been led to believe disappoint or anger God and/or people. This will mean that, in presenting the *question* to children, it is important to move clearly from sin as individual acts to the basic situation that underlies those acts, and conversely, from the fact of estrangement to its actualization in individual acts.

In addition, concrete thinkers are only beginning to appreciate intentionality in evaluating action, as opposed simply to reckoning whether an adult figure approves or whether any damage has been done. It is important to help the children deal with the fact that sin permeates all that they are, even those aspects of their lives of which adults approve.

Children experience being treated as objects by others and are likely to identify this as wrong. However, while they also in turn treat others as objects, they may find difficulty saying what is wrong with this treatment of others. This is because, even by age 10, children do not have a well-developed conscious concept of "living" and "dead" and therefore find it difficult to distinguish between their treatment of things and of people.[36] Similarly, while we adults are familiar with the idea that the sting of death is sin, children will not be likely to appreciate this "sting" to any great extent until after the 10th year when the permanence of death is more readily distinguished.[37]

One aspect of sin which will be a challenge for any teacher to present to concrete-thinking stage children is the fact that we ourselves can do nothing to overcome it. Children usually assume that the "bad" person must change herself—that is "fair." God should punish the bad persons and reward the good (defined in terms of people who do what God wants). That is also fair.[38] To forgive freely a bad person would not be fair at all, from the point of view of typical childhood reasoning. Your task as teacher is to present the question in a manner that calls for the answer to come from outside the child, as gracious gift, unearned and undeserved. And yet, also to present the personal responsibility for sin and our inability to overcome sin by our own efforts.

In analyzing the *question* with concrete-thinking children, we must be sensitive to the legalistic orientation and often self-condemnation that are typical of this age-group, and so we must present guilt and responsibility in a manner that opens the way for the children to hear the message of God's gracious and merciful acceptance, not in a manner that will drive the children to despair. In other words, we must present law in a way that leads to Christ, not in a way that merely focuses on law itself. The good news must always be central in our teaching.

A further challenge in teaching children is to help them identify themselves as the sinners. Usually children assume that they are the good people of whom God approves while others are the bad people whom he punishes. Stories need to be structured so that the child identifies, not with self-righteous onlookers, but with the sinful person who is transformed. This means that stories must clearly present the feelings of a central figure who is not heroic. Children in the later elementary years enjoy stories of heroes[39]; in such stories the hero is the central figure who provides the answers or deals with the problem. In teaching the gospel, the "hero" is actually God. Yet, stories cannot be told from God's point of view—we do not want to give children the impression that we have access to God's mind and thoughts. Nor do we want the child to identify with God as hero, but rather with the human figure who cannot deal with the problem and who is the recipient of gracious healing.

James Fowler reminds us that not every child finds it difficult to identify with the sinner. Some children, due to mistreatment or adult disapproval, have an excessive sense of badness.[40] It is important to know your class well. If some children have a deep sense of disapproval, then the *question* must be presented sensitively so that the children are opened to the answer and willing to believe that no one is so bad that he or she is beyond God's love, that forgiveness is possible for him or her.

Since concrete thinkers are still formulating classifications and have difficulty with gross generalizations (such as all humankind), we may expect that they will proceed slowly in the understanding that all people of all times and places are sinful. Be content if your students grasp that the good news is for them and for those people they know and love. Further growth in generalization will occur in adolescence. Meantime, a personal response to God in faith is the heart of the matter.

In addition, children may resist the idea that all Christians are sinners. Even if the child is willing to acknowledge her own need of healing, she will usually assume that most Christians, especially grownups, are good people who are always on God's side and of whose behavior God usually approves. Or, the child may hold that at the very least, Christians must be less sinful than non-Christians in order for God to love and care for them and allow them to be members of the church! Therefore, you will need to include narratives about persons whom the children will readily identify as "friends" of God who also show clearly the need for forgiveness.

The "fall" narrative in Genesis 3, while a wonderful story for adolescents and adults, is not really helpful in teaching children. This is because literal-minded children tend to historicize the fall as something that happened to two persons called Adam and Eve long ago. But the central theme of the fall is a description of the human situation of estrangement, a description of the way things are for all fallen human beings in this world; it is an affirmation that this fallen situation is attributable to humanity and not to God. With children it will be more helpful simply to state this affirmation rather than use the Genesis story since the story will have the very reverse effect for literal-minded children—it will lead them to assume that the really responsible human beings were Adam and Eve, not themselves!

Ways to express the "question"

When teaching the *question* with the tool of transformationally-structured narrative (Chapter 5), theological terminology can be developed from events in the stories. Definitions will be grasped more easily by children when related to concrete instances.

Keep theological terminology to a minimum. In experimental teaching sessions, only one traditional term—*sin*—was used with children.[41] (Estrangement was considered a less familiar word, even though class "definitions" reflect the notion of estrangement.) From these experimental lessons come the following "definitions" of *sin*. They are examples only. You and your class will need to develop your own definitions from the content of your lessons.

From stories came the following definitions:

Sin—Things were wrong between Mary and God
                                 Mary and people
                                   Mary and the kind of
                                      person she knew she
                                      should be.

Sin—Peter put himself first before Jesus, before God,
       before others. He put himself in the center.

Then, more generally:

Sin—things are wrong between us and God
                               us and people
                                us and the kind of people
                                we know we ought to be.

Sin—self is in the center instead of God.

Additional ways of expressing sin included:
- We are not the kind of people we want to be or that God wants us to be or that people want us to be;
- Although we love Jesus and want to believe in him, we let him down in many ways;
- Something is very wrong in our lives;
- We can't change ourselves and other people can't change us either; we need to be changed by God.

Children and the "answer"

The figure of Jesus is attractive to children from a young age, and older children see him as hero. In presenting the *answer,* be sure to emphasize Jesus and also the new state of things, the healed being, which he brings. Present Jesus as One in whom there was no estrangement between him and God, others, or his own self. Yet, present Jesus too as one who was truly human—who lacked bodily security, was lonely, misunderstood, and so on. Narratives must witness particularly to Jesus' acceptance of others in spite of who they were and what they had done. They must witness to the experience of the presence of new life in people's lives, and to the believing reception of Jesus as the Christ.

In presenting the *answer,* our approach must always be soteriological, so that the children do not merely learn certain things about Jesus, but grasp the transforming and healing work which he accomplished and still accomplishes. We have as our goal that the children will come to faith and personally experience healing, forgiveness, grace, acceptance. Of course, such faith is the work of God and cannot be structured through stories or a program. But, by choosing appropriate narratives, and structuring them in a way that unlocks the meaning of the gospel for the child, the Word may genuinely be heard and the Spirit's work of faith may occur.

As you teach, keep in mind the following points:

One of the most central and difficult aspects of the *answer* for the child will be that of grace. We have said that the late concrete-thinking child relies on the principle of reciprocity as fairness in constructing relationships. Justification is directly opposed to the law-oriented works-righteousness of the age-level. In Luther's terms, we could say that the child is well-acquainted with the legalistic knowledge of God; the Christian educator's task is to communicate the gospel through which the child may learn the evangelical knowledge of God.[42] Therefore, first it must be absolutely clear that the answer to the child's existential questions must come from God alone and not from any other person or thing in the world that they know (including themselves and what they do). And second, it is essential that they grasp God's acceptance of us *in spite of* the fact that we are unacceptable. If the children can grasp this much, and know that God's acceptance is due purely to his love which we do not deserve (that is, his grace), then we can hold that the basic communication of the *answer* has been accomplished. In all of this, we must communicate an understanding of faith as not *doing* anything but simply accepting God's acceptance of us. In faith we respond to God by loving and trusting him with everything that we are.

Since, in presenting the *question* you will emphasize personal responsibility for sin, so equally important will be emphasizing genuine forgiveness and healing in presenting the *answer.* Children are often "let off" punishment just because a parent forgot about the incident or a sitter forgot to mention the misdemeanor to a parent. The children must be aware that God does not merely "forget" about sin but rather genuinely forgives and accepts in spite of what we are like and what we have done.

Since legalism is typical of the age-level, you will want to be very sure that the children have grasped God's acceptance without our doing anything to earn it, before you deal with good works as a response to God's loving acceptance of us.

It would be easy for children to assume that, once accepted by God, a permanent transformation has taken place in the life of the believer so that he or she never sins again. It is important that children learn that forgiveness is not a once-in-a-lifetime experience but an on-going experience; that new life in God's presence is not life without estrangement, but rather assurance that God's forgiveness is always available and that they can daily ask for and receive it.

In using stories with children, be sure to relate the child's experience to the portrayal in the narratives. Help relate stories of Jesus' acceptance, for example, to the child's own experience. Help the child grasp that God's acceptance is unconditional in a way that the acceptance of parents, teachers, and friends can only point to. Help the child sense that God's forgiveness heals the hostility, conflict, and guilt which are repressed and unconscious but very real. Show the children that they can be recentered by a sense of the forgiving divine presence that is always with us.

Be sure that you give children help in relating God's acceptance to their everyday experience. Puncture discussions with questions that will make the children think, such as, Have you ever felt the way that Peter did? Why? What did you do? How would you feel if . . . ? Have you ever known someone who . . . ?

We have mentioned the self-condemnation of abused and rejected children. Even nonabused children sometimes experience long-held grudges on the part of parents or teachers, and judge themselves harshly in turn. It is not easy for children to understand that God forgives even when significant adults in their lives continue to condemn, or that God accepts even when those they love the most reject them. Nevertheless, while this may be difficult to grasp, it is also very much good news for the child. We must show that God's acceptance in no way depends on the acceptance of other people—or even on the children's own acceptance of themselves.

Finally, in teaching children it will be tricky but important to help the children both experience faith as their response and yet to recognize it as God's work. Something that may be helpful, in addition to discussion, is prayer—an actual address to God that calls for total trust in him for forgiveness, or an address thanking God for that trust.

Planning lessons

It will be best to have a series of at least four and preferably more sessions in a unit on God's gracious acceptance. A six-session unit works well. Children need several weeks to absorb the new ideas. There are many aspects of the *answer* to grasp; over a period they can be introduced gradually. It may, for example, take several sessions for the children to move from legalism to grace. In addition, several weeks will allow more time for personal appropriation of the gospel.

Be sure to structure your objectives so that you add new aspects sequentially. Also endeavor in every session to have a whole-person approach. Some of your objectives should be cognitive (to help the children grasp that Jesus accepted Zacchaeus in spite of who he was and what he had done, and that this acceptance made a total difference in Zacchaeus's life). But some should call for personal response to Jesus the Christ (to help the children learn that they can pray to Jesus Christ when they experience estrangement and that he can and will accept them). And some should call for feelings (to help the children rejoice in God's forgiveness). Include objectives that reflect experiences of acceptance in the classroom also (to help the children feel accepted in the class by teacher and peers).

Evaluating whether your goals have been met will not always be easy. Some of the ways you can check will include verbal responses and discussion, written responses, creative activities, written and oral prayers, enthusiastic participation in activities and in devotions, concentration in story time, peer acceptance of and comments on others' work, group spirit, and sometimes even the interest shown by regular attendance, early arrival, and staying late after class. All of these may reflect a thirst for and a response to the good news.

Ways to express the "answer"

In experimental sessions, the words defined with the children were *forgiveness, grace,* and *faith*.[43] These words were called *handy-words* (that is, short-hand words to say quickly what the stories said). Definitions were developed from events in the transformational narratives and later generalized to include the children.

For example:

Forgiveness—God accepted Mary, took her, and loved her, in spite of what she was like and what she had done.

Grace—God's love that Mary didn't deserve.

Faith—Mary trusted and loved Jesus with all that she was. She happily believed that God forgave her.

Then, more generally:

Forgiveness—God accepts us, takes us as his own, and loves us, in spite of what we are like and what we have done.

Grace—God's love that we don't deserve.

Faith—trusting and loving God with everything we are; believing that God forgives us because of Jesus.

Other examples of expressing the answer:

- Jesus came to make lives new and to help people believe in God's love for them.
- Jesus is always ready to give us a second chance no matter how much we feel that things are wrong between us and him.
- Jesus knew that people needed to hear the good news of God's love for them in spite of the kind of people they were.
- Jesus cared about people, and so their lives were changed.
- Jesus was the special person whom God sent to make life new and different.
- Jesus makes things right again for people, he makes things new; he makes us right again, he makes us new.
- God loves us and is kind to us even though we don't deserve that love and kindness.
- God treats us as if we were as good as Jesus even though he knows that we are not.

73

Again, these are examples only. You and your pupils will need to draw your definitions from the stories, discussion, and activities in your class sessions.

Chapter 5

TEACHING WITH TRANSFORMATIONAL NARRATIVE

What is the best way to communicate the gospel to children? There is evidence that narrative is a very important means of communicating with children in the concrete-thinking stage. So we shall explore this means. James Fowler points to the importance of narrative at what he terms the "Stage 2" level which corresponds to the concrete-thinking stage, both as a means of communicating to the child and of the child communicating his or her own experience.[1]

The work of Dr. Richard A. Gardiner also substantiates the importance of narrative for communicating with elementary children. Gardiner has done extensive therapeutic work with children, successfully using a mutual story-telling technique with clients from six years of age onwards. He shows that through narrative children can appropriate new learnings and behavior patterns which might be difficult to communicate in other ways. He also shows that children are capable of structuring their own narratives and of showing their appropriation of the new learnings in their narratives. We shall illustrate below that both of these findings are useful in teaching the gospel as children learn of God's gracious acceptance that is relevant for their lives and structure their own narratives to express their learnings.

In Gardiner's technique, the child makes a recording as "guest of honor" on a make-believe television program on which stories are told. The child then makes up a story from scratch and ends by telling the "moral" of the story, the latter often significantly revealing the fundamental psychodynamics of the story.[2] The therapist then has a turn at developing a story; he uses the characters, setting, and initial situation in the child's story but has a more appropriate resolution of the conflicts. The story thus provides the child with more alternatives, new avenues that the child has not hitherto considered. The therapist's "moral" also emphasizes the healthier adaptations which have been communicated in the story.

In teaching the gospel, you can use stories based on the existential questions of children that also introduce the healing message of the gospel. As lessons proceed, you can expect that the children will become more skilled at communicating through narrative.

Gardiner does not just allow children to ramble on. He instructs the children beforehand that there is a structure to the story—it must have a beginning, a middle, and an end. In teaching also, it is important that stories have a clear structure. The teacher can't simply ramble on!

Gardiner also elaborates on a single primary theme when relating the story.[3] In teaching, we also should resist the temptation to "teach everything" in one narrative. A clear point to each story will be helpful. Not every aspect of justification can be told in one story. But you can build on previous concepts, story by story as the lessons progress.

Structure in narrative

Structuralists distinguish between form (or structure or grammar) and content (semantic).[4] We might say they look for patterns in stories as opposed to the content of the stories. So, for example, two stories might be about different people in different places, but have the same pattern. All of us are familiar with the simple pattern of the television detective drama—the hero is presented with a murder to solve; the murderer foils the attempts of the detective for a while; the detective has a few misadventures on the way; and then, in the last ten minutes of the program, the detective brilliantly outwits the murderer and calls in the police just in time to carry off the villain. This pattern we would call the *structure* of the narrative. Of course, the villain and the heinous crime and the setting change week after week. The hero may even get a new hairdo and employ new assistants. But the pattern remains the same. Some of us even switch channels for part of the show, knowing almost to the minute when to switch back to catch the final climax to the story. We know the pattern.

Anthropologists who are structuralists look at the structure of myths and customs in less-developed societies, seeking patterning of relationships that are typical of the human race.[5] Building on the work of Claude Lévi-Strauss, Elli Köngäs Maranda and Pierre Maranda researched folklore and mythology by examining the units or elementary constituents in narratives and the grouping of those units.[6] On the basis of their analysis, Maranda and Maranda arrived at a set of four models of narratives, one of which exhibits the pattern that will help us in teaching the gospel to children.[7] Put in general terms, this pattern or structure is as follows.

First, there is a problem situation. An agent (a) seeks a solution through inadequate means and fails to solve the problem. Then agent (b) seeks a solution, but, unlike (a), uses an adequate means opposite to the inadequate attempts of (a). (b) thus participates in the function that (a) set out to accomplish. But (b) does so in a successful way. And this in fact reverses the situation for (a) who is enabled to participate in the successful solution provided by (b). In fact, the final solution turns out to be a gain for (a) and the outcome is greater than a mere reversal of the problem. (b) in this outline may be called the *semantic mediator*— the agent by which the solution is accomplished.

Another way of describing the pattern would be: a seeking or scanning phase by Tom which fails to produce a solution; the intervention of an outside agent, Sue, in which the solution is given by Sue's successful participation in Tom's function; a new perception by Tom of the situation in which Tom perceives the solution and participates in it; and a final phase in which Tom recognizes and operates in the light of the solution. In this case, Sue fills the role of the semantic mediator. We shall see below that this structure corresponds to the transformational pattern described by James Loder.

Now, the interesting thing for our purpose is that Elli Köngäs Maranda, under the auspices of the Harvard Center for Cognitive Studies, experimented to establish the development of the mastery of different types of narrative structures in childhood.[8] She used children from six to twelve years of age, and told folktales that were too long for the children to memorize by rote. To retell the stories, the children needed to master the rules of the narrative structures. She found that children from nine to twelve years of age were able to conserve the structure of the more complex narratives, the structure described above. The actual thinking processes involved are similar to, or a little more complex than, analogy. Normally, elementary children cannot perceive analogy or metaphor, let alone more complex items. One would expect that the meaning would be trapped in the story, the structures "concealed" in the narrative. However, clearly, the children were able to perceive the structures when given the stories in these particularly structured forms. It has also been found that as early as five years of age, children respond therapeutically to transformational narrative.[9] Working with children in Philadelphia, it was found that children from eight and a half to eleven years responded well to the teaching of justification using the transformational pattern.[10]

In structured transformational narrative, then, we have a tool that can help the concrete-thinking child grasp the narrative structure in a way that illuminates the content and makes it graspable for the child. The child cannot analyze the human situation philosophically and theologically. So, instead of dealing with justification on an abstract cognitive level, you can use narrative to raise the *question* of estrangement and the *answer* of God's acceptance in Christ. Fortunately, structuring such narratives is an easily learned educational device and can be used by any teacher.

The transformational process

James Loder describes the transformational process in detail. He believes that the process is inherent in human developmental stage transition.[11] The prototype of transformation in the physical development process is transposed with effectiveness to higher orders of behavior—first, to the level of intentional acts of creation in many spheres where the absence of established frames of reference calls for the employment of transformational logic, and then to the level of fictive time in the plot of transformational narratives.[12] It is a pattern deeply ingrained in human experience which the child will recognize. Of course, such experience will not have been consciously reflected upon by the child in terms of the transformational pattern. But, through transformational narrative we shall maximize the possibility of the child experiencing consciously and cognitively the pattern of experience that he or she is already going through and has gone through many times before. In other words, we shall help the child to become intentional about that which is already part of his or her experience. But, our teaching will not have this intentionality as an end in itself. Rather, the use of the pattern or structure in the narrative will be to point beyond itself to the message of God's gracious justification as *answer* to the child's *question* of estrangement. Our goal will be for the children to hear the good news of God's gracious acceptance and to respond in faith as they perceive that acceptance is the true answer to their deepest needs.

The transformational pattern

In depicting transformation as the inherent pattern or grammar of the knowing event, Loder describes five steps. The first is conflict, an apparent rupture in the knowing context.[13] We want to set the rupture right. The second step is what Loder terms the "interlude for scanning," in which the knower searches out possible solutions, takes apart errors, keeps parts and discards others.[14] This step deals with the comprehensive implications of the conflict and looks for a solution in the most universal terms. The third step is the "constructive act of the imagination." This insight or intuition or vision conveys the essence of the resolution.[15] It is a turning point in the knowing event which transforms the elements of the ruptured situation and gives a new perception or perspective to the knower. In the knowing event, this step provides discontinuity, a sense of mystery. Since it is an insightful solution, it has a gift-quality, an element of surprise.[16] The fourth step has two elements—the release of the energy bound up in sustaining the conflict, and an opening of the knower to himself or herself and the contextual situation.[17] The fifth and final step is the "interpretation of the imaginative solution into the behavioral and/or symbolically constructed world of the original context."[18]

Loder's central thesis is that human transformations must themselves be transformed in encounter with Christ.[19] Conflicts that lead to deep spiritual transformation are conflicts that bring us face to face with non-being or the "Void" which "has many faces such as absence, loss, shame, guilt, hatred, loneliness, and the demonic."[20] Only by the transforming work of the Holy Spirit who brings us to conviction in faith can such a conflict issue in transformation. To use our earlier terminology, the *question* can only be answered by God who brings renewal, restoration, and healing by grace.

The transformational pattern is sufficiently compatible with the *question* and the *answer* so that the gospel can be communicated through such a narrative structure. Of the five steps, the *question* corresponds to the conflict and scanning steps. The third, fourth, and fifth steps of the pattern call for radical intervention from outside of the human situation which negates the Void and leads to new self-understanding and the convictional knowing of faith. These steps in narrative will present the *answer* side of the correlation in which new life in Christ overcomes estrangement and brings acceptance and healing by grace through faith as gift.

Our task then, is to plot transformationally structured narratives using the five-step transformational process described by Loder. Most critical in structuring narratives to communicate the gospel will be the role of the "code-breaking semantic mediator" (to use a structuralist term) to enable the learner to apprehend God's gracious forgiveness. This is the role of agent (b) and Sue in the earlier illustrations. In our narratives the "semantic mediator" will also be the theological mediator, Jesus Christ, who brings salvation as gift in accepting the unacceptable and restoring the estranged.[21]

Congruence of form and content

We have seen that children can grasp the transformational pattern or structure of narrative. But what of the content? Unlike anthropologists, we who teach the gospel cannot ignore the content. It is critical! How can the child grasp the content? The answer lies in the congruence of form and content in our transformational narratives.

If Loder is correct, the structure of transformational narrative actually bears the pattern or "grammar" of the Holy Spirit who transforms our situation, negates our negation or the Void, and brings us to the convictional knowing of faith which involves a new understanding of who we are and a new way of being and living. The pattern of the narrative actually points beyond itself to the message that it is intending to convey.

Consider the Maranda and Maranda pattern. An agent seeks a solution but cannot find one. The solution comes from outside, through another agent who participates in the function of the first, but does so in a way that accomplishes the solution of the problem. Then the first agent participates in that solution and in an outcome even greater than simply nullification of the initial problem situation. To put it even more simply, the transformational structure involves a pair of opposites and a "semantic mediator" capable of including them. While this structure is neutral as far as content is concerned, we who teach the gospel can fill it with the content of the gospel message. For example, if the first agent is understood as humanity, and the second as Jesus Christ, then the *question* and *answer* of estrangement and acceptance would read something like this: Humanity in the situation of estrangement sought many a solution (legalistic, and so on) and failed to find an adequate answer to the human predicament. Human beings could not solve the existential situation. The answer to our predicament came from outside of the situation in the person of Jesus the Christ who came into the human situation and did for humanity what humanity could not do for itself. He sought a solution that was truly adequate to the problem of sin and accomplished it once and for all successfully—indeed he was, in himself, that solution. Thus, humanity can now participate in that "solution." The final outcome through Jesus the Christ is not merely a reversal of our initial situation, but true forgiveness and indwelling by the Spirit, so that persons through faith can participate in new life and indeed be truly a new creation.

This crossover pattern or chiasmic structure (from the Greek letter chi, χ, which has a crossover shape) is expressed many times in Scripture to refer to the salvation brought by Christ. Consider the biblical formula, "For our sake he made him sin to be sin who knew no sin, so that in him we might become the righteousness of God" (2 Cor. 5:21). Or Paul's image in Romans 8:1-2—humanity under the law of sin and death could not provide a solution, but "God has done what the law, weakened by the flesh, could not do: sending his own Son in the likeness of sinful flesh and for sin, he condemned sin in the flesh" (v. 3). The result, says Paul, is that the just requirement of the law has now been fulfilled in us and we no longer walk according to the flesh but according to the Spirit; we are no longer under condemnation (vv. 4, 1). Or again, consider the imagery of Christ as the New Adam who reverses the effect of the Old Adam (Rom. 5:12-21, 1 Cor. 15:22). And so we could go on.

The Cross itself is often referred to in chiasmic terms— through Christ's identification with sinful humanity, subjecting himself to death on the Cross, he is able to accomplish for us that salvation which we could not accomplish for ourselves. In Tillich's understanding of the Cross and Resurrection, Jesus the Christ participated under the conditions of existence and experienced its ultimate negativities; he was victorious over the existential estrangement to which he subjected himself, and so in faith, we are reunited with God from whom we were estranged and share that victory. Or again, by participating in human existential estrangement, Jesus, who was never estranged from God, others, or himself, effected his saving work and so saves us from our old being of estrangement and its self-destructive consequences.[22]

By structuring narratives with this pattern, children are able to grasp the "transformation" of their human situation from one of guilt and unacceptableness (about which they can do nothing) to one of forgiveness and acceptableness to God by grace alone through faith alone.[23] Jesus will be the one who spans both sides of the formula, the symbol through whom the message is grasped. When developing such narratives, the transformational structure needs to be very clear: the person's dilemma of estrangement; Jesus' identification with the person and acceptance of the person in gracious love; the person's acceptability in Christ in spite of being unacceptable; the person's new status of forgiveness, new standing as accepted, new being in the Spirit; the effects of the gift of faith in the life of the believer. However, a structure by itself is not magic. Whether or not the child will respond in faith does not only depend on whether he or she perceives the structure and content of the narrative. It is the work of God the Spirit to elucidate the questions in the human situation and to provide the answer through the Word of the gospel. As teachers, the most that we can do is to structure narratives carefully, together with other classroom experiences, so that the *question* and *answer* are presented as clearly as possible. But, ultimately, we must rely on the Spirit for the children to hear the Word of the gospel and truly respond in faith.

Perhaps a word of warning is in order. We were reminded in Chapter 2 that symbols can be demonic. Transformational narrative in religious education fulfills a symbolic function—it points beyond itself to God's ultimate transforming forgiveness by grace received in faith, which gives the believer a new situation of acceptability in spite of his or her unacceptableness. If the transformational pattern in narrative communicates this message so that children respond not to the narrative itself but to God's saving activity in Christ, then the transformational narrative will indeed be an agent of healing. But symbols can point to themselves. If we become absorbed in the structure merely for its own sake, and the children simply marvel at the structure as an interesting phenomenon without hearing the message, then the narratives will serve a demonic function.

Transformation analyses of biblical narratives

Following are analyses of two New Testament stories according to the transformational pattern. Formal structural analyses of these and other stories, using the pattern of Maranda and Maranda, are in the appendix.

Zacchaeus

[Jesus] entered Jericho and was passing through. And there was a man named Zacchaeus; he was a chief tax collector, and rich. And he sought to see who Jesus was, but could not, on account of the crowd, because he was small of stature. So he ran on ahead and climbed up into a sycamore tree to see him, for he was to pass that way. And when Jesus came to the place, he looked up and said to him, "Zacchaeus, make haste and come down; for I must stay at your house today."

So he made haste and came down, and received him joyfully. And when they saw it they all murmured, "He has gone in to be the guest of a man who is a sinner."

And Zacchaeus stood and said to the Lord, "Behold, Lord, the half of my goods I give to the poor; and if I have defrauded anyone of anything, I restore it fourfold." And Jesus said to him, "Today salvation has come to this house, since he also is a son of Abraham. For the Son of man came to seek and to save the lost."

Luke 19:1-10 RSV

The question

Zacchaeus is initially satisfied with himself as one who puts himself and his needs in the center of his life, indicated by his taking inflated taxes. He is, of course, unacceptable to the populace. However, there is conflict—perhaps barely conscious—in Zacchaeus's life. He wants to see Jesus. No reason is given, but clearly there is a desire to see the Christ which is more than mild curiosity. In fact the desire is strong enough for convention to be cast aside. Zacchaeus climbs a tree in public in order to see Jesus. Alienated from the populace, Zacchaeus is also alienated from the person he himself wishes to be. He both accepts himself as he is—and at the same time seeks another who differs from him and whose life-style condemns his self-centeredness. This seeking represents the "scanning" phase of the transformational process, although Zacchaeus's grasp of his problem is dim if indeed it is conscious at all.

The answer

Then Jesus comes to Zacchaeus and shows his acceptance of him by inviting himself to Zacchaeus's house. Jesus accepts the person who is unacceptable. In that moment, Jesus himself becomes unacceptable to the crowds. And, in the same moment, Zacchaeus experiences acceptance on a level he has never known before. He experiences grace as the gift quality of free acceptance. Jesus accepts him *in spite of* who he is. Thus, Zacchaeus experiences the essence of justification by grace.

The initiative in the story lies with Jesus who seeks out the estranged one and in the seeking allies himself with the unacceptable. Zacchaeus could not transcend or change his situation. Even in seeking to see Jesus, there is no indication that Zacchaeus had any idea of the radical change that might result from meeting Jesus.

The encounter with Jesus does not begin Zacchaeus's conflict, but it brings it to the fore. Zacchaeus is now faced with the person that he is. He recognizes his situation as it truly is. Only too clearly, he understands himself as the alienated and estranged one whose self is in the center of his life, who has accrued goods for himself at the expense of others. According to the narrative, Jesus does not verbally explain the situation or pronounce judgment. His presence is the judgment; in himself he is the Word both of judgment and of acceptance. As Zacchaeus is faced with the question of his existence he realizes that his hopes for his future have been based on the false assumption that accruing goods for oneself will result in happiness. Zacchaeus's plans and hopes for his future are brought under judgment as he is faced with the One who is centered in others and their needs, including the very needs of Zacchaeus himself. Zacchaeus's false hopes are thus shattered in the moment that he is claimed in acceptance, love, and friendship by Jesus. Or, in other words, the existential *question* of estrangement and the *answer* of the new life in Jesus as the Christ are revealed simultaneously. There is no lengthy period of repentance. Rather, as Zacchaeus grasps the question he is already experiencing the answer. And the very acceptance both reveals his unacceptableness while it empowers him to accept his new self given by Jesus in the moment of acceptance. Jesus' acceptance is the sole basis for the transformation of self-centeredness and alienation into other-centeredness and restoration.

Zacchaeus's whole system of values is turned upside down. The puzzling fragments of his life come together. He is opened to know himself in a new way. What has previously been an acceptable life-style and has hitherto defined who he is now becomes abhorrent to him. Zacchaeus thus seeks congruence in his life with the person he now understands himself to be—graciously accepted and loved by Jesus. And so, he wants to give of himself to those he has defrauded, instead of taking. He pledges to give away a large percentage of his riches, including a fourfold restoration of that which has been taken fraudulently.

The key in the whole experience is the coming of Jesus who, as mediator, both exposes Zacchaeus to who he is (and so reveals his unacceptableness in the very act of accepting him) and gives power for change in Zacchaeus.

Peter's denial and restoration

Simon Peter said to him, "Lord, where are you going?" Jesus answered, "Where I am going you cannot follow me now; but you shall follow afterward." Peter said to him, "Lord, why cannot I follow you now? I will lay down my life for you." Jesus answered, "Will you lay down your life for me? Truly, truly I say to you, the cock will not crow, till you have denied me three times."

John 13:36-38 RSV

Simon Peter followed Jesus, and so did another disciple. As this disciple was known to the high priest, he entered the court of the high priest along with Jesus, while Peter stood outside at the door. So the other disciple, who was known to the high priest, went out and spoke to the maid who kept the door, and brought Peter in. The maid who kept the door said to Peter, "Are you not also one of this man's disciples?" He said, "I am not." Now the servants and officers had made a charcoal fire, because it was cold, and they were standing and warming themselves; Peter also was with them, standing and warming himself.

Now Simon Peter was standing and warming himself. They said to him, "Are not you also one of his disciples?" He denied it and said, "I am not." One of the servants of the high priest, a kinsman of the man whose ear Peter had cut off, asked, "Did I not see you in the garden with him?" Peter again denied it; and at once the cock crowed.

John 18:15-18, 25-27 RSV

When they had finished breakfast, Jesus said to Simon Peter, "Simon, son of John, do you love me more than these?" He said to him, "Yes, Lord; you know that I love you." He said to him, "Feed my lambs." A second time he said to him, "Simon, son of

John, do you love me?" He said to him, "Yes, Lord; you know that I love you." He said to him, "Tend my sheep." He said to him the third time, "Simon, son of John, do you love me?" Peter was grieved because he said to him the third time, "Do you love me?" And he said to him, "Lord, you know everything; you know that I love you." Jesus said to him, "Feed my sheep. Truly, truly, I say to you, when you were young, you girded yourself and walked where you would; but when you are old, you will stretch out your hands, and another will gird you and carry you where you do not wish to go." (This he said to show by what death he was to glorify God.) And after this he said to him, "Follow me."

John 21:15-19 RSV

The question

During the Last Supper, Peter declares that he is willing to sacrifice his life for Jesus. But Jesus knows that Peter is over-confident of himself and predicts Peter's threefold denial that very night. As a matter of fact, it will not be Peter who lays down his life for Jesus, but Jesus the Good Shepherd who lays down his life for Peter.

There is no question about Peter's devotion and intention to be loyal. Nevertheless, although Peter and another disciple follow along to determine what is happening during Jesus' trial, Peter denies that he is Jesus' disciple when confronted by the maid and then others in the courtyard. In other words, Peter's prime loyalty is not to Jesus but to himself. And so, when self is threatened, he preserves self at the expense of denying his Lord. This raises to Peter's consciousness an understanding of himself that he had thought impossible—in fact, one he had emphatically rejected in his protestations of loyalty to Jesus. The Void opens before Peter as he sees who he is. And there seems no hope of forgiveness or restoration. Jesus is already in the hands of the authorities; it is clear what the outcome will be. Staring Peter starkly in the face are despair, disillusionment with himself, estrangement between himself and the person he knows he should be (and that he has claimed to be), estrangement between himself and God's emissary the Christ, and therefore, between Peter and God himself. Peter's world has collapsed. The One who gave meaning and purpose to that world not only is no longer with him but has been separated from him by Peter's own disloyalty and selfish concern. Peter cannot recompose his world.

The scanning phase for Peter includes a more constructive approach than that of Judas who, in his moment of self-revelation and self-hatred, destroys himself. Peter's solution apparently is to return to the company of the disciples as they gather again after their scattering. The story does not tell us of Peter's inner search for a solution in the days following the crucifixion.

The answer

The solution to Peter's dilemma comes at the initiative of the risen Christ. The Lord takes Peter aside and in a threefold restoration not only accepts Peter as friend but gives him a commission to serve the believers. In spite of Peter's disloyalty, Jesus restores to Peter the task that he had earlier been given. Forgiveness is expressed in the strongest of terms by restoration of the relationship and by the responsibility entrusted to Peter. Peter is treated as if he were a trustworthy follower in spite of his actions and words to the contrary.

As the Johannine church knew and proclaimed, the risen One is the One who was crucified. The One who was broken on the cross is the One who takes Peter's brokenness and shattered world and self into that brokenness of the cross. Peter's disloyalty and self-condemnation are negated by the loyalty of Jesus the Christ to Peter (and to all of his followers) as he hangs rejected and denied yet constantly loyal and accepting of those who deny him. And so he is the One with power, the only One who can heal the estrangement between Peter and himself, the only One with power to restore Peter as the loyal and loving disciple. The Void for Peter is transformed. The victorious One is victorious not only over the Void in general but over Peter's own particular

Void of estrangement and guilt and self-rejection. Jesus transforms Peter's situation from self-centeredness to Christ-centeredness, revealing Peter's sin for what it is and showing himself as the One who has power to transform and to make new.

As James Loder describes it, the structure of the transforming intuition works as follows: "human intention, self-defeating in its negation of divine initiative, is negated by divine intention. Cancellation is the result of this double negation such that human intention is now left free to choose for the Author of the cancellation."[24] Peter's experience of guilt and self-rejection is negated by the divine intention of the One who was crucified and suffered for those who denied him. Peter is now free by the gift of gracious love, forgiveness, and acceptance to choose for Jesus as the Christ and to respond to his invitation to loyal service. Jesus' threefold approach to Peter is both judgment (shown in Peter's grief at being asked three times to affirm his love) and an opportunity for new life. Peter is assured that he will indeed remain faithful even to death as he had once vowed—but now because of the grace of the risen Lord, not because of his own self-certainty. In acceptance, Peter learns who he is—not the braggart leader but the forgiven one who is loved and trusted in spite of who he is, and who is called to serve those who are also accepted by the Rejected Crucified One. The call and its empowerment are at the initiative of the Christ, and so are part of the context of grace.

Choosing narratives

There are some criteria to keep in mind when you are choosing stories to communicate justification.

First, ask yourself, Do the stories indeed genuinely communicate the *question* and *answer* of estrangement and acceptance, of sin and forgiveness? Do they show God's gracious initiative in salvation and the believer's response of faith? No matter how exciting or interesting a story, if it is not theologically sound, do not use it.

Second, if you use Bible stories, be sure that as far as possible you use them in the way in which the author intended. Not that we can ever get back to the original author and ask what that intention was! But good Bible commentaries can help in indicating the meaning of the text in the light of its context, and can suggest whether the story was used within the early church as a narrative to communicate salvation. Twisting biblical narratives to achieve an end—no matter how worthy an end—is never an acceptable practice. And fortunately there is no need to do so. The Bible is full of wonderful narratives that communicate the gospel.

Third, ask yourself whether the structure of the story and the content converge—whether both structure and content show the extraordinary acceptance shown by God in justification. In choosing the stories, clarity of structure is important. Again, we do not wish to twist biblical stories or add to the details in order to achieve the "right" structure. Fortunately again, the Bible has many stories that indeed do have the fivefold transformational pattern (pp. 79-80). Of course, if you wish to structure contemporary narratives, you are entirely free to structure the five steps as clearly as you wish. Some biblical stories at least would seem to be called for; we do not want the experience of God's forgiveness separated totally from the historical manifestation of God in Jesus the Christ.

Fourth, choose stories that are able to be divided easily after the *question* and before the *answer*. Often in teaching it will be helpful to pause after the *question* for discussion so that you can reinforce the message and check whether the children have grasped it on a personal level. Then you can continue with the *answer* of the narrative and complete the pattern. In testing with children, the pause after the *question* included the opportunity for the children to suggest how the story should end—a legalistic response typical of the age level was expected and received in the initial sessions. Following the *answer* section, the children retold the ending so that the teacher could tell whether the children's perception had changed.[25]

Fifth, be sure that the story shows clearly Jesus the Christ as the mediating symbol who brings about the "victory" ending in the story.

Sixth, choose stories with which you think your students will identify. The elucidation of the *question* must be one to which the child can relate. This does not mean that you cannot use stories about adults. Most biblical narratives are, in fact, about adults. But the human problem must be expressed in a way that the children can recognize is true also of them. For some stories, a figure might represent the typical law-orientation of the imperial child, for example, so that the child is faced with the radical graciousness of the answer in contrast to legalism. Like the question, the answer also must be one that the children are able to incorporate into their personal story.

Seventh, attempt to have stories about both males and females. While any human being can identify with any genuine presentation of the human question, children are helped when they can identify with someone of the same sex, at least occasionally.

Eighth, select stories that will help the child appreciate not only the transformation brought about by the "visible" Jesus on earth but also that wrought by the "invisible" Lord whom the child experiences. Children are closely tied to that which can be seen and touched. They may well suppose that the visible, earthly Jesus who could be seen and touched would be able to work transformations in people's lives long ago but that he can no longer work today since he can no longer be seen or touched. It is important that children learn the power of the risen Christ to transform lives now and that they believe that their own lives can be changed by him. Stories from the book of Acts as well as stories from church history and contemporary stories will be helpful for this purpose.

Ninth, choose a story for its simplicity of message. In teaching the gospel, there is only one message that you want the child to wrestle with and to believe—God's gracious justification of the sinner. This abstract notion will be communicated through the structured narrative. But you want to avoid adding difficulty to difficulty. You may want to avoid, therefore, stories that involve additional metaphor and analogy. Parables may best be saved until the stage of formal operations since they involve metaphor as well as the message. To "unpack" the parable of the prodigal son, for example, the child must deal with two levels of difficulty—first, identifying the mediator in the story as the father and relating the father's gracious activity to the activity of God, and second, dealing with amazing acceptance in spite of estrangement. You may be able to use transformational narrative to unpack the metaphor as well as the plot and content. But you may also find that this twofold task is asking too much of one tool. The concrete child may fail to understand the metaphor and conclude that transformation is a human activity. On the other hand, some scholars have found that transformationally-structured parables work well.[26]

If you are teaching just one student, you could probably follow Richard Gardiner's lead, and let the child begin telling stories of her experiences or problems. Then you could conclude the story with an acceptance narrative. Such an approach would ensure the interest of the child. But, if you are teaching a group of children, this approach probably will not work. The children will have different experiences, and some may select situations that do not describe estrangement. It will be simpler to use a previously-structured narrative to present the *question*.

Children's structured narratives

When children have grasped the transformational pattern—usually after several lessons—they are able to verbalize it. Then, if you wish, you can encourage the children to develop their own narratives. This procedure will have two-fold value. It will help you determine if the children really have grasped the structure and message. And, it will give opportunity for the children to make up narratives about a make-believe child their own age and sex—with whom you can assume that they will identify. In this

93

way pupils can express God's gracious intervention in making things new for children. If your own structured stories are mainly about adults, the latter point will be particularly valuable.

Telling the stories to children

The biblical stories above were analyzed in adult terms according to the transformational pattern. Clearly you will not use this terminology with children. Following is the way the Peter story might be told to children.

The question

Today's story is about Simon Peter, one of Jesus' disciples. Peter had been a loyal and trusted friend of Jesus during the years when Jesus traveled from town to town telling people about God and caring for their needs.

Now, Jesus knew that the time had come for cruel people to arrest him and kill him. Jesus decided to have a last meal with his friends. And during the meal, Jesus began to prepare his disciples for what was about to happen to him.

Peter, strong, loyal Peter, promised Jesus that he would stand by him even if it meant that he would die. "Lord," said Peter, "I'll die for you!" Oh, and he meant it! He'd do anything for Jesus, anything to protect him, anything to be his loyal friend.

But Jesus knew Simon Peter very well. He knew that even the most loyal of his friends would not stick by him. "Tonight," said Jesus sadly, "before the rooster crows in early dawn, you will say three times that you aren't my friend."

Now, I'm sure that Peter was determined that such a thing would never happen. But—when Jesus was arrested that night by soldiers in the Garden of Gethsemane, most of his disciples ran away, scared for their own safety. Peter was a little braver than they were. With another disciple he followed Jesus and the soldiers from a safe distance. They went into the courtyard of the high priest's building, while the soldiers took Jesus inside. And then it happened! A servant girl recognized Peter.

"Hey, you're one of Jesus' disciples, aren't you?"

"Oh, no," cried Peter. "Not me."

He quickly moved away from her to the charcoal fire where he could get warm. But the servants and officers around the fire recognized him right away! "You're one of Jesus' disciples!"

Peter began to panic. "No, no! I'm not!" he shouted.

"But I saw you in the Garden of Gethsemane with Jesus," accused a servant.

"No, no, no!" said Peter. "Not me. I wasn't there. I'm not a friend of Jesus at all." The only thing that Peter could think of was—himself and his own safety.

And just then, in the dim light of morning when the air was so still, a rooster began to crow. Oh, Peter remembered. He remembered what Jesus had said. He remembered his own empty promises. He had not stood by Jesus at all, far less died for him. He had let Jesus down. Peter crept away, bitterly disappointed in himself. He knew that he had done something that God would not want him to do. And he had never felt so bad about his relationship with Jesus—things were wrong between them because he had betrayed his friend. Peter wasn't the person he ought to be or even that he had promised to be.

So many times Peter had heard Jesus tell people they were forgiven. How he wished that he could tell Jesus how bad he felt. But, it was too late to tell Jesus anything. Already the people in charge of the land had decided to put Jesus to death. Peter knew that he had failed. And there was no way to tell Jesus how sorry he was.

(Break for discussion on what Peter might have thought and felt, followed by discussion of times we might have thought or felt like Peter.)

The answer

Good news! Although Jesus was crucified, that wasn't the end. On Easter Sunday, Jesus came back to life again. That evening, he met with his disciples, but Peter didn't get a chance to say anything privately to Jesus.

But a few days later, Jesus met Peter and six of the disciples in Galilee where they were fishing. He helped them catch fish and they all had breakfast together on the beach. I wonder if Peter raised his eyes during breakfast? How ashamed he must have felt.

After breakfast, Jesus took Peter aside. He knew what Peter needed. Peter could not make things right between himself and Jesus. But Jesus could! Jesus knew that Peter needed love that he didn't deserve. And Jesus always had plenty of love. Peter needed forgiveness; he needed Jesus to accept him in spite of what he was like and in spite of what he had done. And Jesus did just that. He gave Peter a second chance.

"Simon," said Jesus, "Do you love me?"

"Yes, Lord, you know that I love you."

"Then take care of the people who will love and trust me and believe in me."

Phew! It was over! But no—Jesus asked a second time, "Simon, do you love me?"

"Yes, Lord. You know that I love you."

"Take care of my people."

Peter was feeling pretty uncomfortable. Wasn't it over now? But there was the question again: "Simon, are you sure that you really love me?" Wouldn't Jesus believe him? Peter said, "Lord, you know everything. You know that I love you. I really, really do."

And Jesus said, "Take care of my people. Teach them and look after them. You know, the day will come when you'll stand up for me right to the point where you will die for me. Meantime, you be my disciple."

So Peter was forgiven and received a second chance. Three times he had denied knowing Jesus. Now he had been given three opportunities to say how much he loved Jesus. And three times Jesus told him of the important job he was giving him. "I'm forgiven. I'm still his disciple! He's going to let me be a leader among his people after all," thought Peter.

And Peter did become a great leader and preacher. Soon he was telling about Jesus to thousands of people. In the years that followed, many people came to love and trust Jesus because of the things that Peter told them about him. Legend tells us that he was indeed killed years later because he was a faithful disciple.

(Break for discussion on what Peter might have thought and felt when Jesus gave him a new start; talk about how we ask for forgiveness and a new start.)

Chapter 6

GOOD NEWS
FOR YOUTH

There are particular opportunities and problems that face the teacher of youth when communicating the gospel. In Chapter 1 we mentioned Sally's concerns: young people's ideas sometimes seem to be as peculiar as those of children; sometimes the teacher of adolescents feels that she is unteaching most of what the students have learned previously; and then, when the students do get going on the right track, they often seem to take two steps forward and three backward!

Unteaching misconceptions

Sally is describing what often literally happens in teaching adolescents. And it is a phenomenon that we should expect. In childhood, students do not receive information passively and store it away quietly until old enough to understand it. Piaget showed us that the child tries to make sense of what he or she hears. By the process of assimilation she relates new information to what she already knows.[1] If the new information does not fit previous schema, then she will accommodate her thinking to fit the new information. (Shannon sees an animal and assumes that it is a dog. Then the animal purrs and meows. This doesn't fit her concept of a dog. She asks what the animal is and is told it is a cat.

Now Shannon has a new concept, that of "cat.") But, what if there is no one to tell Shannon that the animal is a cat? What if she simply adapts her conception of "dog" to include animals that purr and meow? Or, what if the person she asks gives her false information? Shannon will then have a misconception to be unlearned later. Even more confusing, the person may give an explanation that makes no sense to Shannon at all—that the creature "is an entity of the feline species." Then Shannon may conclude that asking questions gets you nowhere, and that whatever the animal is, it is really a concern for adults, not children.

Much of our teaching of the Christian faith is rather like this illustration. Eight-year-old Shannon hears the term *justification* in a Bible reading or hymn. She may simply assimilate the term to her present knowledge. "God gives us justification," Shannon thinks, and breathes a silent prayer thanking God for giving her family "just a vacation" in Florida. Or, Shannon may ask a teacher or parent what the word means. The well-meaning adult may try to explain the concept by substituting a word that he thinks is more familiar. "Oh, it's another word for salvation," he replies. This really does not help Shannon at all because she doesn't know the meaning of *salvation* either. She begins to get the message that asking adults doesn't help; this is probably something that is not for children to understand. Or, the adult might try an explanation in simpler words, not realizing that this does not really simplify the concept at all. "Justification means God pronouncing us to be just," replies the parent. The words may be simpler, but Shannon still has no idea what the parent is talking about. Sadly, and perhaps even more likely, the parent may respond, "I don't know. Ask the pastor sometime!"

What happens, then, when Shannon joins your eighth grade Sunday school class or appears in a catechetical class? She already has some thoughts about justification. And they are confused at best. Or they may be a mixture of error and boredom. All this Bible jargon never did make sense, she thinks.

You actually do have some unteaching to do. Whenever you teach youth, especially in early adolescence, it is probably safe to assume that there will be unlearning that needs to take place. But youth are very self-conscious and easily embarrassed. They do not want to attract attention as the "dummy who always says something stupid." So, unless you intentionally check on their understanding, you may wrongly assume that your students understand your terminology when in fact they do not. Even they may assume that their understanding is correct! And so you constantly talk past each other. Checking misunderstandings can be frustrating and humiliating for adolescents if done in the wrong way. It can become rather fun if an element of humor is introduced. You might turn the humor on yourself. "When I was a kid, I had this funny notion about salvation. I thought it was spelled with an *e* and had to do with selling." Students may share their understandings if they think that you too have made mistakes. Once the students recognize the inadequacy of their previous notions they are ready to learn new understandings. If you do not go through this step, adolescents will continue to hold their old assumptions. Of course, sometimes you may find that there is no need for unlearning. But often students will have many misconceptions and unteaching will take some time.

Slow progress in early adolescence

How about the "two steps forward and three backward?" In early adolescence, abstract thinking is an exciting new tool. But it is also a difficult and sometimes a frightening one. The adolescent who, in the childhood years, has conceived of God with a physical body that looks like a movie star finds that thinking about God as spirit is possible but alien. The comfort of the old way of thinking is attractive. When tired or depressed or simply inundated with too much that is new and unfamiliar, adolescents will revert to the concrete thinking they used for so many years. Don't be surprised at this. It is completely normal. And, it isn't really three steps backward although it may seem that way to a frustrated teacher. The young person is simply sending a message saying, "Slow down. Let me go at my own pace for a while."

The wise teacher will revert to concrete categories until the youth is ready to go on. With a number of adolescents in a class reverting to concrete thinking at varying times, it may seem as if there is never a good time to "go on." By all means go ahead, but review often enough so that the adolescent who is "resting" in his or her old mode of thinking still has the chance to catch up when he or she is ready. Patience is a virtue in most tasks, but in teaching adolescents, it is an absolute requirement.

Remember too, that individuals vary in their development. Most persons reach the age of formal operations, and therefore are capable of propositional thinking (necessary for formal theological reasoning), about the age of 11 to 12 years. Even then they probably need some time to practice abstract thinking before they are ready for the complexity of many doctrinal formulae. But not everyone has the same timetable. Some persons reach the stage of abstract thinking earlier. And some may reach it considerably later. This does not mean that there is anything wrong with them. There is a range in the developmental schedule that is absolutely normal. What this means is that, even when most of the class seem to understand technical terms and theological reasoning, there may be one or two students who are struggling desperately. One way for a student to deal with boredom and frustration is to become a discipline problem—a manifestation you will not want in your classroom! Nor will you want to frustrate students and make them think they will never be able to understand the Bible. Transformational narrative will be a helpful tool in teaching the gospel to these students. If the students feel that they are apprehending some of what you are teaching—and if they grasp that they are apprehending the most important, personal aspect—then they will feel less frustrated. In addition, allow for individualized approaches to learning so that students may proceed at their own pace.

Because of the speed with which students develop and practice abstract thinking once their brain cells have matured to this point, there can be a decided difference of ability and pace in thinking in the early adolescent years. Unless you plan to individualize extensively, it will probably be helpful to limit your class to a specific age group rather than mixing too wide a range of grades. Once students have reached the age of fifteen or so, you can expect that most will definitely be using abstract thinking, unless they are mentally impaired. So, from 10th grade onwards, you can probably mix grades successfully for conceptual learning. Of course, there may be social factors that will make you want to deal with ages separately even in later adolescence.

Define terms carefully and simply in the early adolescent years. Let students use them in sentences and practice developing what amounts to a new vocabulary. Frequent review is necessary in teaching adolescents; new terms and ideas take many repetitions before they are fully learned.

A new way of teaching catechetics

What happens if your students have already been introduced to justification by means of transformational narrative in childhood, as suggested in Chapter 5? This will make your catechetical teaching much easier. It will mean that you already will have something on which to build. And you can use the technique of transformational narrative to review previous learnings and to introduce new ones.

The students will have appropriated justification as God's acceptance in spite of the fact that they are unacceptable; they will have grasped and responded to the message of a gracious God communicated through transformational narrative. This experience is genuine and deep. But it does not do away with the need for more technical theological teaching in the teenage years once the stage of abstract thinking is reached. Rather, it prepares the way for such teaching. What has been taught to concrete-thinking children in narrative form will now be formalized. Your function as a catechetical teacher will be quite different from that envisaged by a theorist who would delay the communication of doctrine totally until the adolescent years. In the latter approach, you would actually be introducing justification for the first time. Or, you might consider yourself "unlocking" that which has been "trapped" in narrative for years. But, if the children have been introduced to God's gracious acceptance through transformational narrative in the preceding years, your catechetical teaching will rather be labeling in more mature ways that which the children have already experienced and known in narrative form. You will be reinforcing in a new and adult way that which is familiar and dear to the students, and you will also add more complex aspects of the faith.

The tried and true principle of teaching from the known to the unknown would suggest that you might best begin teaching about salvation with some of the narratives with which the students are already familiar. This will have the benefit of review, but also give a genuinely devotional atmosphere in which to teach. The good news will be presented in a way that is eminently personal. From there you can proceed to label and formalize in mature and more traditional ways those things which the students have already learned and experienced—namely, God's gracious acceptance of them in spite of their self-centeredness and estrangement from God, others, and themselves. Rather than teaching that which is totally new, the catechetical classes will highlight and reinforce the experience of God's grace appropriated in the concrete-thinking stage. Catechetics will develop further vocabulary to help the students in expressing their experience, such as the term *justification* itself which will probably not be used with children. And, catechetics will help the students to express in formal, abstract terms their appropriation of grace.

By beginning with transformational narrative, you will have common ground for all of your students. Not every one will go on to the depths of history of doctrine. Some may be mentally challenged and remain basically at the concrete-thinking stage; they will appreciate the transformational narratives. Even students who develop sophisticated theological reasoning often appreciate the opportunity to express in story their understandings.

TEACHING THE GOSPEL TODAY

Helpful hints

In teaching youth use technical theological language as seldom as possible. When you need to use it, explain that technical language is simply helpful shorthand. Instead of saying, "God accepts us freely out of love and forgives us through Jesus the Christ in spite of our hostility and estrangement and putting ourselves in the center of our world, and our response is a matter of accepting that gracious acceptance," it is quicker to say, "God justifies sinners by grace through faith." Seen in this light, most teenagers readily accept theological terms as a useful way to save time and words. They may liken technical terminology to mathematical formulae which can say a great deal in very few symbols. Be sure that you explain terms carefully and that they are thoroughly understood. To learn the "shorthand" without really grasping what it stands for is of no real help to the student. He or she then proceeds to become a teacher who in turn passes on the terms without explanation, and so confuses further generations of students.

In teaching more traditional and technical theological material, you have some work to do before even getting into lesson plans. First, summarize for yourself the traditional terms and theological arguments that you want to convey. In Chapter 3 we did this already in general form for adults today. You might want to look through Chapter 3 and select those aspects that you think will be most appropriate for your students. Second, begin to categorize the concepts in terms of their difficulty. The simplest things to teach are those that are concrete—that could be perceived in principle by sight or touch or hearing or taste or smell. (For example, There was a man called Jesus who lived two thousand years ago. Jesus was crucified.) Then ask, what is the simplest and what is the most difficult of the rest of the understandings you might want to teach. Ideas that involve gross generalization and that are far removed from the adolescent's own person are probably the most difficult—for example, cosmic salvation in relation to the universe and eschatology. Save these more difficult concepts until later in the teaching process.[2]

Consider which learnings can be taught by using analogy or metaphor. Analogy and metaphor are graspable by abstract thinking and fascinate the adolescent. They are also wonderfully rich ways of expressing beliefs. Parables are an excellent tool for communicating God's love and acceptance. What could be richer or more beautiful than the parables of the prodigal son, the lost sheep, or the lost coin (Luke 15)? Teenagers can appreciate the metaphorical thinking involved in parables and can appropriate the message as personal good news.[3]

You can also use traditional imagery from the Bible and the church's wrestling with beliefs through the ages. Theories of the atonement, for example, are really pictorial images. Whether we see Jesus on the cross marching to wage decisive war on the forces of evil (Christus Victor) or whether we view his work as that of sacrificial lamb and so on, we are using rich metaphorical language. With early teens, just one or two images or "theories" are all that they can handle in complexity. As the teenage years proceed, by all means introduce the many additional images that are used in the Scriptures and in church history.

Developing more complex ideas

As the students gain facility in using abstract thinking, you will want to deal with doctrinal aspects of the gospel that may have been touched on but not fully developed in the childhood transformational narratives. Atonement and Christology are clearly among these. By ninth or tenth grade most students will be ready to "put together" the Christian faith and relate doctrines to one another. The student will be ready in a more sophisticated way to relate who Jesus was to what he did. The middle to late teenager can appreciate some of the struggles of the early church in dealing with these issues. They can pinpoint similar struggles today in arguments between denominations and sectarian groups.

Some of the more complex issues that students may appreciate late in ninth grade or in tenth are as follows: God's acceptance leading to our acceptance of selves and of others; the *in spite of* element of God's acceptance; the dialectical relation of law and gospel; Christ's suffering and obedience for sin; the cost of salvation; the need for daily repentance and return to grace; the whole-person quality of faith; the fact that all human beings are equally sinful in God's sight and that Jesus alone was sinless.

You will also want to help students in mid-adolescence wrestle with the complexities of our being simultaneously creatures of God and sinners, and also of simultaneously being saved by grace and yet also sinful and in need of daily repentance. Youth may grasp this as a personal reality yet still raise painful questions about others. They may ask in disillusionment, "But how could my parents have done such a thing? I thought they were Christians. Why didn't God stop them?" Such questions are not easy. But youth have the mental ability to appreciate the role of human freedom in sin and to place the responsibility on human beings, not God. They can also appreciate the complexity of God's omnipotence together with grace that allows humanity the freedom to be sinners.

In middle adolescence (15 to 18 years), students enjoy the complexity of relating their basic understandings to the way in which others perceive the gospel. What do other denominations believe? How do different groups of Christians understand the relation between justification and works? Between justification and a personal decision for Christ? Between salvation and baptism? And so on.

By later adolescence, students usually want to explore even further—what do other religions believe? What have people historically held to be salvation? Is an atheist's position tenable? For this reason, we find parents sometimes associating what is happening socially in their children's lives with what is happening intellectually. "Going to college has turned my Robert into an atheist," cries Mrs. Lithgow, not realizing that college has little to do with it. Robert is simply exploring options—and perhaps stating his independence of parents at the same time by shocking them with statements that challenge the beliefs that they have always attempted to teach him.

However, some adolescents of college age cling fiercely to traditional teachings and do not wish to explore other views. In effect they ask for stability and security to support them as they face approaching adulthood.

Middle and later adolescents often also ask serious questions about the practical implications of belief. Should my faith result in action? And, if so, what action? Deep ethical and social questions may be faced as students wrestle with these issues.

Deepening commitment

As the teenager is able to think in a new mode, so the "whole picture" of God's work for us becomes clearer to the student. Often, the teenager experiences an intensely personal response to God as this whole picture forms. This does not mean that the person did not have strong faith as a child. But, the expression of the child's commitment changes as the faith-in-search-of-understanding finds that understanding. To say that the person is now a Christian would be wrong. All baptized persons are Christians. But, the teenager may experience a newness of such intensity that he or she may claim that it is as if they have not "really known God before." (Some denominations call this conversion, but it is certainly a different phenomenon from the person who hears the gospel for the first time and responds.) These young people now have an opportunity for renewed rejoicing in belonging to Christ's church and in daily repentance and renewal in the gospel.

The teenage years therefore are important for developing personal devotional practices.[4] How to pray and to read the Scriptures are skills that can be taught and practiced both in the class or group setting but also in private. Daily journaling and other meditative practices may be introduced as ways of reflecting on God's grace.

You may use transformational narrative in helping students express their experience of God which is deeply and personally intense. Structuring their own story enables the students to reflect upon that experience. Youth are even more capable than children of developing their own narratives. Such narratives may be shared or they may be written in a journal for personal use only.

Some youth tend to overemphasize their own response to God. To avoid the impression that God's justifying love rests on *our* commitment to Christ, be sure to emphasize the primacy of Christ's commitment to us. Our commitment is response to his commitment. And our commitment is a gift from him.

Youth and the "question"

How do youth experience sin and guilt? Clearly, one answer will be, the same way that you and I do. But, there are certain experiences of adolescence that will be helpful in focusing the *question* for youth.

Early adolescence particularly is a time of centering on the self. This is due partly to the new capacity of thinking which enables introspection. It is also due partly to the social-emotional question of "Who am I?" In a society that sends conflicting signals to youth as to when they can seriously be considered adults, the question of "Who am I?" looms large. This focus on the self means that sin in terms of self-centeredness will make a great deal of sense to youth.

On the other hand, in later adolescence the young person is concerned about wider social and ethical issues, and also is developing deeper personal relationships often with members of the opposite sex. Then, sin as corruption of the whole universe and human society and culture can be emphasized, as well as sin in terms of broken relationships.

David Elkind draws attention to youth's experience of stress today.[5] Due to their abstract thinking ability, adolescents experience a new emotion—worry. They worry about themselves and the difficulties associated with puberty. Guilt and anxiety are associated with new sexual desires. They also worry about the future. In class discussion such worry and guilt are likely to be expressed.

Youth also experience estrangement from peers. The peer group is very important in adolescence,[6] especially in early adolescence when it begins to replace the authority of the parents and provides a support group for the individual as he or she develops independence. David Elkind points out that estrangement from peers is likely to be experienced by youth in terms of peer exclusion due to social prejudice, peer betrayal and exploitation, and the shock of disillusionment as idealized figures that are the object of teen crushes fall from their pedestals.[7] Beware lest youth express this estrangement only from their own point of view, as rejection directed at them by others. Help students also to acknowledge the times they have been the perpetrators.

Youth also experience estrangement in the family setting. Adolescence is a period of developing independence from parents. This move to self-determination may be accompanied by disruption, conflict, and anxiety for both adolescents and parents.[8] In addition, the increase in separation and divorce in the last two decades adds to the pain of discussing estrangement in families.[9] Some adolescents may feel guilt, anger, and hostility in relating to separating or divorcing parents.

Youth may also express alienation and disillusionment from an adult society that exposes teenagers to insecurity and stress by increasingly eroding markers that used to confirm youth in their progress toward adulthood.[10]

Be especially sensitive to students who have had traumatic experiences of estrangement such as physical or sexual or emotional abuse. In many cases victims blame themselves or assume unwarranted guilt. Distinguish between the guilt that all of us bear as members of the human race and to which the gospel is addressed, and the psychological guilt that needs therapeutic treatment.

The above experiences are reflective of estrangement between youth and themselves or youth and others. You must help youth to move from their estrangement in these experiences to the depth of sin which is estrangement from God. Youth's ability to think abstractly can enable them genuinely to appreciate estrangement as broken relationship with God. They can grasp that such estrangement is basic, and that all other estrangement derives from that alienation. Adolescents can also deal with the complexity of a God of love who is also a God of wrath and judgment, and who condemns sin yet loves the sinner.

Due to abstract thinking, stories that have a "hidden" meaning, such as parables, make sense to the young person who can now grasp the metaphorical meaning. The Genesis story of the fall will have meaning for the teenager in a way that is not possible for children and is an excellent means of communicating sin as elevating ourselves to the place of God.

Youth and the "answer"

In early adolescence, as abstract thinking enables the young person to conceive of spirit and so of God as spirit, we said that God may seem alien from the God conceived in childhood. It will be important to emphasize the personal characteristics of God which the young person has known and loved for so long—and which are the essential message of the gospel—God's love and forgiveness and caring, yes, and wrath and judgment.

When teaching early adolescents, keep in mind that they are coming out of the legalistic stage of later childhood. We have seen in Chapter 5 that transformational narrative helps in communicating grace to the child whose natural tendencies are to legalism. Transformational narrative may do the same for legalistic youth. Be patient if your youth find it difficult to grasp God's graciousness. After all, history gives testimony to the difficulty that multitudes of adults have had with the same issue.

One characteristic of abstract thinking is the ability to introspect. This ability may cause youth to focus long and hard on their sin and guilt. It is most important that the law lead to Christ and that youth understand repentance as a means of reaching out in trust to God's grace in Jesus. Concentrate on the objective work of Christ rather than subjective self-assessment. Over-self-examination can itself be a form of works righteousness (earning God's favor by superrepentance) to which youth are prone.

Youth's introspection results in self-consciousness. Focusing on their physical and emotional changes and new thinking powers, youth become self-centered. David Elkind proposes that adolescents then assume that everyone around them is also concerned with the thing that so fascinates them—themselves![11] Elkind calls the assumption the *imaginary audience* and says that teenagers feel that they are always on stage playing to this audience. Such focus on the self means that youth will resonate to the specialness of the gospel "for me." The wonder that Jesus died for me will be an appropriate emphasis for teenagers.

By middle to late adolescence, youth are developing deeper relationships with peers and are especially interested in relating to persons of the opposite sex. The developing intimacy will make this period an appropriate time in which to present justification as restored intimate relationship with God. Reconciliation and forgiveness will be felt deeply.

In adolescence persons must come to terms with their permanent physical appearance. Children often hope that when they grow up they will be as beautiful as a princess or as attractive as a male movie star. In adolescence, as the body comes to full maturity, the individual is faced with the fact that he or she resembles a grandmother or uncle or parents much more closely than the movie star. It will be important to balance this disappointment in self—often aggravated by the ability to introspect and the hours spent in front of the mirror—with the fact that God does not value the adolescent in terms of physical beauty but rather simply because of God's own unconditional love. This is good news even for the adolescent who is not overly disappointed in his or her appearance. Media give constant messages about the desirable appearance and standard of youth. It is good news to know that worth in God's eyes depends on Christ alone. And that all of us are part of God's good creation with our diversity, as opposed to the single image the media may project as ideal.

In the bewildering and stressful time of adolescence, the stability and lack of pressure in the gospel are good news for youth. Elkind reminds us that today's youth are pressured into

111

adult responsibility.[12] Parents, media, school, and peers all place stress on the adolescent.[13] The gospel is one area of life that is stable—the good news does not change, even though society's demands may be constantly changing. And, the gospel is the least stressful aspect of our lives—it is the one area where hurrying and doing well just does not apply. There is literally *nothing* at all that youth can do to earn God's favor. Nothing! Youth may be pressured by parents to obey rules, by school to earn good grades, by peers to earn sports trophies and get dates, by the media to look like models or sports heroes. But God says, Don't *do* anything. Don't hurry! Don't be stressed! Just accept the fact that it's all done already in Christ for you! Such news is very good—but hard to believe—for youth who are daily pressured to do and do well.

The main task of adolescence is achieving independence. As the young person breaks free from dependence on parents, the gospel indicates that there is good dependence too. Healthy dependence on God for grace and forgiveness and Presence in time of need must be distinguished by the adolescent from childhood dependence on adults. The gospel also calls to interdependence in the community of believers, interdependence rooted in the One who proved ultimately dependable on the cross. Adults who show concern for youth, listen to them, give time to talk and be with them, and above all who witness to the centrality of their own faith will be role models for youth. Their acceptance of youth can become an analog for God's acceptance. Their dependence on God for forgiveness is testimony that maturity includes reliance and trustful dependence on God.

The peer group provides help for the adolescent in the struggle for independence. But it also brings its own pressures. Youth need an integrated personality to resist peer pressure. The power of the Spirit integrates the personality. Prayer and reliance on the Spirit should be very important elements in the lives of teenagers. In addition, Jesus' resistance to group pressure in accepting those who were unacceptable and in facing the cross can be helpful symbols to communicate Jesus' power to youth.

The issue of identity is of great importance to the adolescent. Who am I as a developing, independent person? The gospel answer is quite different from the answers received from the "mirror" of other persons' responses. I am a child of God; I am a person loved and valued by God in spite of the fact that I am a sinful human being; I am a person claimed by God for all eternity; I am a person with whom God is present at all times; I am a person who doesn't need to do anything to earn God's love because he has already given it to me and gives it to me constantly; I am forgiven. For youth in times of doubt, the identity question is answered as it was with Martin Luther—I am baptized. The "in spite of" quality of justification needs to be part of the young believer's identity. In spite of what others think of me, in spite of my self-condemnation, in spite of rejection at home, and, above all, in spite of my undeserving, I am loved and claimed by God. In this is an identity worth having!

Youth are moody, due to hormonal changes and to social pressures. The gospel is the news that God is not moody! God does not change his mind about us on whims, one day condemning and the next loving, as peers may do. God does not give us conditional love one day and apparently unconditional the next, as parents may do. God does not accept us when we are in a good mood and reject us when we are angry and depressed as society may do. God's love is constant, unconditional, unfailing. More good news for teens!

God's love for all people can be grasped conceptually by adolescents due to formal operational thinking. But many early teenagers find it difficult to talk about God's love for those unpopular individuals whom the peer group rejects. It almost seems as if an admission of God's love for the unpopular person is an act of disloyalty to the peer group, an admission that the person "isn't so bad after all." Young adolescents often define their peer group negatively as "we are not people who are like this unpopular person." So, an admission of God's love for the unpopular one can be tantamount to weakening the definition of the peer group.

To aid young teens, help them define their group positively; having common goals is a mature way to define a group. ("We are the people who do. . . ." "We are the group who plans to. . . ." "We are the group that likes to. . . .") This will help remove the need for scapegoating and so make it easier for young teens to admit God's love for unpopular peers.

Work patiently with youth who, through emotional or social crises, find the notion of God's love for all persons difficult to believe. We have mentioned victims of physical, sexual, and emotional abuse. An abused teenager may first find it difficult to believe in God's love for him or her, due to misplacing of guilt on the self. Once the victim has managed to lay blame at the door of the abuser, he or she may find it almost impossible to believe that God's love and forgiveness are available for the abuser also. Professional counseling may be helpful.

Testing

Some teachers give tests and grades on theological and biblical information, especially in the early adolescent years. There are pros and cons to this practice. The pros are those that one would associate with any testing of learned material—it ensures review of that which was learned, it gives feedback to the teacher on areas that were misunderstood and need further teaching, and it may give the student a sense of satisfaction in having accomplished so much and in having recognition for that accomplishment.

However, there are serious points to be made against testing. The most dangerous lies in a misunderstanding of the gospel. The students might relate the test grade to his or her worth in the sight of God or of the church. If I get a good grade then God will approve of me; a bad grade and God will disapprove. To obviate this danger, it may be wise to avoid testing altogether. But, if you do decide to use tests, discuss with the class beforehand how testing will help you in your teaching and help them in their learning. Point out many times that a test has nothing whatever to do with the way in which God or the church or you as a Christian view the student. God accepts us in Christ in spite of our sin and that is *the* important issue. Passing or failing tests is a distinctly secondary issue and has absolutely no relation to salvation at all. While this may seem obvious to you it is not at all obvious to teenagers without careful and frequent reiteration.

Another danger is that testing can put too much emphasis on the cognitive appropriation of the gospel at the expense of emotion and volition. Since all aspects are involved in faith, it is important that we do not unwittingly emphasize one over against the others. Again, to avoid this danger, it may be advisable to avoid testing or to do it as little as possible.

Chapter 7

GOOD NEWS
FOR ADULTS

Adults and the "question"

We have already dealt extensively with the *question* in Chapter 3. Adults are capable of grasping all of these aspects in a whole picture.

The most important thing for adults is to keep the personal emphasis. Adults are experts at asking questions to which the gospel is not the answer. We will do anything necessary to avoid being confronted with God's judgment and salvation in Jesus Christ. We want to justify ourselves.[1] In justification, God reveals that we are unacceptable and accepts us freely, declares us guilty and forgiven, tells us we can do nothing and then does everything for us. Sinful human beings do not like the first part of each of those phrases. We do not like being revealed as unacceptable! We do not like being pronounced guilty! And, perhaps most of all, we do not like to think that there is absolutely nothing that we can do to save ourselves. In the learning setting be prepared, therefore, for all of those intellectual arguments to justify themselves that adults have given so expertly through two thousand years of history! And be prepared to use the Scriptures to point out their invalidity.[2] All efforts at self-justification fail and so show themselves to be part of the human question—witnessing to our need for God's answer but failing themselves as answer.

Adults today experience estrangement often in terms of human relations. Just as children and youth today are faced with the estrangement of separation and divorce, so most poignantly are adults—perhaps even more so. Daily newspapers scream headlines that adults will use also to express the *question*—corruption by politicians elected to offices of trust, drug dealing, spouse abuse and child abuse, violence, terrorism, and hostility between nations, races, religions, classes. The list, unfortunately, seems endless. Our inhumanity to our race is only remarkable for its ingenuity in devising new and worse means of expression and action.

Adults, if honest, will also express deep despair about estrangement from the selves they know they ought to be. The availability of contemporary counseling services often helps adults achieve insight into who they are; they may understand estrangement from self in new ways. While counseling can help in the preliminary sphere of psychological and social health, it cannot without the gospel provide the help which adults need at the ultimate level of restored relationships with God. It cannot deal with the depths of self-estrangement that result from estrangement from God. Adults today may have insight into themselves, but it is insight that calls for an answer that psychology cannot give.

As in the case of youth, do not allow adults to dwell only on their experiences of estrangement from self and others. These experiences are helpful in analyzing the human question in the lives of your students, but you must lead on to the root issue of estrangement from God. Estrangement from others cannot really be dealt with until God gives the answer to estrangement from himself by accepting us unconditionally in Jesus Christ.

Be sure to emphasize sin as a state or inclination of human nature. Adults may have had years of usage of the word *sin* as meaning "a bad deed." Such deeply-ingrained, habitual use can only be changed by constant repetition of the broader understanding of sin as inclination of our whole nature.

In addition to the experiences of estrangement common to all human beings, there are particular issues to face at various stages of adulthood that have implications for the expression and analysis of the *question* and that may prove to be helpful starting points for discussion.[3]

Young adults are developing intimate relationships with others. They may experience the betrayal of a broken engagement or disillusionment with an early marriage. In seeking a vision of society with which they can operate in the adult years, they may find the *question* written large in the problems of today's society. In the work force, they may experience estrangement in competition for jobs.

The "me generation" has been with us for a couple of decades. In today's society, young and middle adults will relate to sin as self-centeredness. Often, the first inclination is to identify self-centeredness in others. Be sure that adults are honest about their own inclination to put themselves in the center of their lives instead of God. The story of Adam and Eve is as useful with adults as with adolescents in portraying each person's situation as one of elevation of self to the place of God.

In moving on to midlife, parents are often eager to learn to state verbally what they believe. They are keen to answer the questions of children and adolescents. In parenting teenagers, doctrine may be one of the few discussible topics on which parent and child can agree! Since teenagers like to practice arguing skills,[4] parents will often seek help in expressing beliefs verbally. This has a good and a bad side. The good side is the interest the parent has in learning more of the Bible and theology. The bad side is that such learning may become an intellectual exercise designed to pass on information to children. Be sure that the existential aspect of sin is uppermost, that adults do not merely examine sin "objectively" but rather as those who are deeply and personally involved.

With midlife reevaluation of career choices, married or single life-styles, and ideals, some adults experience estrangement in disillusionment, marriage difficulties, and divorce. In climbing the career ladder, many adults experience estrangement between themselves and the boss, fellow workers, and persons who work for them. They may also experience disappointment in self as they realize that the dreams of their youth will probably never be realized.

Aging or death of parents can bring adults face-to-face with their own aging and death under the conditions of existential estrangement—with what Tillich calls the horror of death and the experience of death as an evil.[5]

Some members of your group may have particular experiences of estrangement through oppression in our society—persons of color, women, immigrants, abused, unemployed, and so on. It is crucial that we listen to their experiences. It is also important in discussion to balance the personal responsibility we each have for sin and the societal structures that need redemption.

From midlife to retirement, many adults have more time for thinking and group learning when children have grown and careers are well-established. There may be more time for reflection on the experience of the human *question*. Death of parents and friends may bring the question to light in new ways.

Older adults continue to experience estrangement through the deaths of relatives and friends. They may also experience estrangement through broken relations with adult children, and through loneliness.[6] Many older persons live by themselves; they may resonate to a definition of sin as being centered on the self. The oppression by society of the older adult is often a way in which estrangement is experienced by senior citizens; systemic hostility and injustice may be starting points for discussion.

Adults and the "answer"

The answer also is outlined in Chapter 3. Consider the points on justification, and also the issues in the previous chapter on youth. Some adults will need to review the same points that high school students may examine. In addition, most adults are ready to deal with even deeper levels of complexity. So by all means discuss Christology and its relation to soteriology. Examine what it means to say that God declares us righteous for Christ's sake. And take a deeper look at atonement—that is, Christ's work by which we are reconciled to God. You may want to pursue additional images of atonement in the Scripture and in theological writings, such as substitution, propitiation, expiation, ransom, satisfaction, liberation, and Jesus' work as mediator, redeemer, and priest. Paul Tillich suggests that in looking at any image or "theory" of atonement we should preserve the following principles: that God initiates atonement through Christ by grace alone; that there is no conflict in God between his wrath and his love; that God does not overlook the depth of sin; that God in Christ participated in existential estrangement and its self-destructive consequences, especially in the Cross, and so transforms them for those who participate in his participation and share in the suffering of Christ.[7]

Adults who seem already to have thought deeply and personally about the gospel message may be ready to explore early church controversies about sin and grace such as that between Pelagius and Augustine.[8]

Drawing out the implications of life under the Cross, with all its complexities of joy and suffering, requires thinking ability that can hold in tension many alternatives simultaneously. While this is not possible with children, it is not only possible but desirable with adults. Luther's belief that justification always results in the Christian's participation in the Cross[9] is a good example of teaching that you will want to reserve until the later teenage and adult years for full appreciation of its depth and implications.

Adults also may raise the question of future judgment and eschatology. Be sure to root discussion of future judgment in the Cross. Justification is our future hope precisely because of God's promise in Christ. God is a God who accepts us in spite of our unacceptableness now and always. Past, present, and future judgment and salvation are rooted in God's redeeming activity in Christ and in the victory already won over sin in his life, death, and resurrection.

Young adults may respond to particular expressions of the *answer*. Their interest in communication skills and developing intimate relations makes them particularly responsive to forgiveness and the restoration of broken relationships. Reconciliation will therefore be an excellent way in which to approach the answer of God's acceptance in Jesus Christ.

Young adults seek a vision of the church and of society with which to operate in the adult years. As the idealism of later adolescence gives way to reality, young adults realize that they may not achieve all that they had hoped for in society or in the church. Important aspects of the gospel for young adults will be the news that God's salvation extends to society and the world, and the complexity of *simil iustus et peccator* as reminder that the church in this world is not perfect.

Young adults seek guidance for their life. They want to know about the practical implications of the gospel for establishing a family, for taking responsibility for finances, for caring for one's health and physical resources.

Since many young adults look to a trusted adult as mentor as they move into mature independence and self-reliance,[10] you have a crucial role in witnessing to your own faith and in being prototype of the acceptance the young adults need.

The *answer* in terms of reconciliation is also likely to resonate with adults on their way to midlife. Many are raising families, and some middle adults will be adjusting to new, blended families from remarriage after divorce or bereavement. In the family, reconciliation is a constant phenomenon. Forgiveness will be a helpful paradigm. Also, acceptance in the marriage relationship and in the family, although part of the human situation and always conditional, can be used as an analog of the divine unconditional acceptance that we all need.

Grace is a valuable theme in midlife. In today's society both men and women are bombarded with society's demand that whatever we get should be earned. We receive wages for work; we pay for goods; we are highly suspicious of anything advertised as free ("Where's the catch?" we ask). Grace goes against our everyday experience. Grace is not, cannot be, earned. It isn't fair recompense for something that we have done; not even our faith is a way to earn grace. God's generous mercy contradicts, therefore, all that we experience daily. Adults need to be reminded constantly that God's free acceptance is the reverse of our worldly experience.

Ethical implications of the gospel are critical issues for adults in midlife. What does it mean to live a life of *agape* love—in the church, in my vocation, in my home, in relation to aging parents, in society, in the nation, as a member of the world which increasingly becomes a global village. Daily baptism and daily repentance will be central. And justification resulting in the justified participating in pain and suffering should also be included.

To know that there is forgiveness for those things which society does not easily forgive or forget is good news to the adult. By midlife most persons have done many things which they regret. They deeply need repentance and a word of grace. In addition, they may appreciate a supportive learning group as they face the reality that God's forgiveness may result in their forgiving themselves but may not always mean that they will be forgiven by family, friends, or society at large.

Faced with grief and fear of death, the implications of the gospel are good news. We have already died with Christ and been raised; that is the news of God's pronouncement of judgment and forgiveness in Christ. Justification was at the root of Luther's belief that with physical death sin will cease, and so he could call death blessed.[11] Justification puts physical death in perspective. This does not mean that adults should not grieve. Grief is a healthy psychological process. But the bitterness and despair of death has been overcome in Christ.

As persons in midlife adjust to lost dreams and ideals,[12] the gospel comes as the good news that God does not count our worth in terms of the promotions received, the dollars earned, and the perfect children raised, but rather in terms of the Cross and our Baptism. As some adults adjust to midlife changes in career or marriage, the stability of God's unchanging love in Christ may also be comforting.

From midlife to retirement adults may be interested in relating the gospel to the social and career authority they may have achieved.

In addition, from about 55 years onwards, many persons show a renewed tolerance or mellowing that allows them to experiment with new ideas; exploring the ways in which other denominations or groups historically have viewed the gospel may give new and rich images and insights.

When children have grown and left home, many adults find renewed interest in relationships and communication as they need to develop communication skills with spouse and adult friends. This may be a good time to deal again with forgiveness, acceptance, and reconciliation.

In retirement, implications of the gospel for stewardship of time and health are relevant issues. The victory of Christ over death, the accepting Presence in loneliness, and the power to heal estranged relationships are all pertinent. Developing deeper prayer and devotional meditation may be possible now that individuals have more time at their disposal. The gospel "for me" is also a helpful emphasis as physical frailty forces attention on the individual's own concerns. The warmth and fellowship of the accepting church matters greatly to older adults who experience the estrangement of society's rejection.[13]

For all adults who experience oppression, rejection, and discrimination due to race, sex, color, age, place of birth, or other factors, the gospel is often most readily perceived as liberation. The practical social implications of liberation in terms of justice call us to action. But be sure that liberation is understood as freedom from estrangement between ourselves and God as well as from injustice between people and social structures.

Narrative for adults

Sometimes we think of stories as tools for communicating with children. Adults, we think, are "beyond" stories. And yet, we face the reality that Jesus told stories with great success to adults, stories that adults have loved to tell and retell since. Societies of ancient times told stories. And, if television viewing is any indication of interest, we adults today enjoy a greater selection of stories than most past generations could have envisaged. Are stories really only for children?

Some writers suggest that narrative is constitutive of the very self, and enables the person to face the truth of his or her existence and to develop self-identity. They hold that narrative organizes experience and gives cohesiveness to life, and that it further helps in relating the person's experience to God's story. If these points are valid, it is not surprising that story is a powerful tool for use with persons of all ages, including adults, and it will be an appropriate and powerful tool in communicating to all ages the gospel which calls us to face the truth of our existence, gives us new self-identity, and relates as answer to our experience of questionableness.

Stanley Hauerwas holds that narrative is constitutive of the self—or rather, narratives are constitutive of the self, for the self consists of many stories.[14] Moral growth, for example, "involves the constant conversation between our stories that allows us to live appropriate to the character of our existence."[15] Hauerwas says that the self is "the formation of character by a narrative that provides a sufficiently truthful account of our existence."[16] He believes that for Christians the story of God as found in Israel and in Jesus provides just such a basis; God's story enables the conversation between our stories to take place in a truthful manner.[17] The unity of the self is provided by "a narrative that charts a way for us to live coherently amid the diversity and conflicts that circumscribe and shape our moral existence."[18] The unity of the self is like the unity of a good novel, with many subplots that help us in dealing with the conflicting loyalties and roles we confront in our existence. The narrative enables us to step back from ourselves and evaluate what we have been doing. What we need is a narrative that gives us skills of interpretation so that we can incorporate our past into our ongoing history.[19] We must be able to give up past false accounts of ourselves and reinterpret who we are. Our "narrative" permits such reinterpretations and maintains a sense of continuity between our past, present, and future.

This narrative has a gift-quality. It is not something that we create. Rather, we are born into a community which is itself the embodiment of a story. This story grasps us through the community and enables us to recognize ourselves in the story that we make our own. We need a true story that provides for us to examine ourselves and enables us to develop our own narrative that can cope with the conflicts of our existence.[20] Christians believe that they have such a story in Jesus Christ. God's story helps us face the truth of our existence. Hauerwas urges us to tell the Christian story in such a way that the hearer is offered a place in the adventure.[21] He believes that the use of stories of Christian saints is helpful in enabling people to reflect on how their own lives exhibit narrative. In addition, Hauerwas encourages the use of stories and novels to analyze dilemmas in life and help us see solutions.[22]

Narrative will be a helpful tool in communicating justification to adults. It will help persons face the truth of their identity (which is a function of the law) and develop their new self-identity (in the gospel). Narratives will aid in analyzing the existential question of estrangement and will help the learners see the solution as coming graciously from God, giving a new relationship between God and themselves and making them new persons. Stories of believers whose lives exhibit the narrative of the human dilemma and God's solution will be particularly appropriate. We have already used such biblical stories in transformational narratives for younger learners.

Hauerwas reminds us that the gospel story is embodied in the Christian community. The classroom or learning group should be a microcosm of that community in living as well as in telling the story that is constitutive of it.

Another writer who gives insights that are valuable for our purpose is Stephen Crites. Crites holds that narrative creates coherence in life, that the formal quality of experience through time is inherently narrative.[23] Narrative is one of the two cultural forms (music being the other) that are capable of expressing coherence through time. It is "one of the ways we organize a life of experience that is in itself inchoate."[24] Folk stories that relate to festal occasions especially lie deep in the consciousness of a people. Sometimes these are not told directly but are ritually reenacted with music. The people's own lives are part of these communal stories; the sense of self and world is created through them. Such fundamental or "sacred" stories are at the root of all the mundane stories that are directly told by a people.[25] Crites suggests that the mediating form between the mundane and the sacred story is the "experiencing consciousness" and "the form of its experiencing, is in at least some rudimentary sense narrative."[26] When mundane and sacred stories and experience cross, we experience luminous moments that we call symbolic. Symbols are the double intersection of the sacred story with an explicit narrative and the course of a person's own experience.[27] In using transformational narrative with any age level, we seek to so structure narrative that the learner will experience a "luminous moment" and recognize gracious intervention as the sacred gospel story intersects with the narratives and with the learner's own experience.

Narrative, then, is an appropriate means of communication with adults as with any other age level. It helps to develop self-identity, organize their world, and aids persons to face the truth of their sinful existence and the questions of the human situation to which the message of the gospel is the answer. Particularly appropriate will be stories of Jesus' effect on the life of believers, told in the communal setting of the classroom or learning group, and with a personal place in the story for the learner. The narratives should intersect with the learners' own experience. We can reinforce this "intersection" through class opportunities for group reflection on the narrative and for creative personal self-expression in response to the narrative (see Chapter 8). In these ways, learners may be enabled more fully to grasp God's justifying activity for them. Their personal appropriation is most important. Adults may easily grasp the transformational pattern and

the correct doctrinal phrases. But we as teachers want to communicate the gospel in such a way that the person is faced with
God's judgment and merciful acceptance in spite of the person's
sinfulness, and is called to a response of faith. Narrative is able
to provide the opportunity for such personal response through the
intersection with the learner's own experience.

Transformational narrative with adults

Is transformationally-structured narrative a helpful tool with
adults? Let's return to Sally, whom we mentioned in Chapters 1
and 6. She noted not only the diversity of adults but also that
some seem to think like children. Now, adults are quite capable
of abstract thinking (except in cases of severe mental impairment).
Most of us use abstract thinking daily, although we may revert
to concrete thinking occasionally. But, as Piaget pointed out,
cognitive development is a matter of nature and nurture, of brain
cell development and of education. The fact is that many persons
in congregations dropped out of formal educational programs in
churches when they were barely in the stage of formal operations.
This means that they have had little opportunity to reflect in
mature ways on biblical content. In many cases, they have very
vague ideas about many theological issues. Childhood misunderstandings are mixed with more mature ideas developed through
hearing sermons or from conversation. Small wonder, then, that
in classes these adults seem to reflect the kind of understanding
that older children may have. In the matter of justification, many
adults left Sunday school when they were in the legalistic phase
of later childhood. Grace made little sense to them at 12. And it
really doesn't make much sense now.

Transformational narrative can be a very helpful means to
enable adults to appropriate God's gracious acceptance. Clearly,
your vocabulary will be different when teaching adults from that
you will use with children. But the five-step structure, with the
division into *question* and *answer,* will be most appropriate.
Moreover, if the transformational narratives are biblical, the technique will have a double advantage with adults: the biblical stories

are genuinely suited to adults—they were written by adults and for adults as the primary readers; and, adults can readily identify with the adult characters in the stories.

As with teenagers, once the *question* and *answer* have been explored through narrative and discussion, the formal theological labels should be attached. Creative and personalized expression may reinforce the message for the learners. Adults may enjoy singing hymns which have meant a great deal to them over the years and which perhaps they now will appreciate in a new light— hymns that include the technical theological terms which they have explored (such as *justified, grace, sin, law, righteousness*). Adults sometimes sing words that they would be hard put to explain if asked; it is a joy when they feel they have grasped the meaning.

Of course, you need not be limited to biblical stories. Transformationally structured narratives based on church history or contemporary experience will also work well with adults and may have the element of unfamiliarity that will raise interest.

For mentally-impaired adults, structured narrative may well be a helpful means of communication. And also bear in mind that all adults in times of trauma or crisis may revert to concrete thinking; at such times a structured narrative may be more helpful than a formal theological discourse.

An additional dimension

With adults, you may add a dimension in transformationally-structured narrative that you may not want to use with children. And this is the dimension of judgment. Children who are developing the logic of concrete thinking tend normally to relate God to legalism and the condemnation of bad persons. To accept persons unconditionally in spite of their undeserving is likely to be considered by the child ridiculous and unfair. Therefore, grace is the emphasis to place on narrative with children since judgment and condemnation will reinforce the child's natural pattern of thinking. The difficulty for the child is not to conceive of God as judge but as merciful Lord.

Now, for many adults the opposite may be true. Theology in some congregations is so watered down that God is seen as a weak being who simply cannot really judge anybody. The Scriptures teach otherwise. God's wrath and judgment are taken seriously by biblical writers. And, indeed, if we don't take them seriously, it is difficult to see what is so special about God's gracious forgiveness *in spite of* our undeserving. Sin is serious business! And salvation is the more incredibly wonderful because of that seriousness.

To this point we have tended to present transformational narrative as a "happy ending" narrative form. But the structure is merely a structure; it can be made to communicate different messages depending on the content. For the purpose of communicating the good news of God's acceptance, it is a particularly appropriate structure as we have seen. But, with different content we could communicate a judgment outcome. It is the content and not the form that determines the outcome as "sad" or "happy." Understandings that you might wish to communicate to adults or older teens include judgment for those who reject acceptance, and the life of the believer as one of suffering, pain, and Cross. The story of the rich young ruler (Luke 18:18-25) could be analyzed according to the transformational structure to show that Christ's effect was not always one of joyous faith, but of rejection and judgment that brings to light the gravity of self-centeredness, sin, and estrangement. The story of Paul or of Dietrich Bonhoeffer, of one of the early martyrs or one of today's martyrs, could be structured to communicate the effect of Christ in the life of the believer in terms of participation in Christ's suffering for others.

Perhaps it is important to note that no tool can be asked to do more than it is capable of doing. Transformational narrative has a simplicity of structure that cannot simultaneously communicate both a judgment ending and a gracious ending, although back-to-back narratives might communicate first one ending and then another. To retain both law and gospel, both judgment and mercy in one narrative, one simply divides the steps into *question* and *answer* as we have seen. In telling an acceptance narrative, be sure to allow for the possibility of rejection of grace. In order for agent (a) to participate in the effective solution of agent (b), (a) must accept (b)'s solution and share in that which (b) has accomplished in order that (a) might have a new and different situation. Each of the biblical narratives in the appendix includes the acceptance of Christ's acceptance, the reception of grace, the faith commitment, without which the ending could not be a new situation for the believer. While this acceptance is empowered by Jesus as the Christ, it is not compelled by him; rejection is possible.

Adults can construct their own transformational narratives and share them with powerful effect. In this way adults not only share their own stories, but also help one another in hearing a Word of grace. In addition, if an adult constructs a narrative that is basically one of personal judgment, group members might offer alternate grace-filled endings. In this way, a person who finds it difficult to believe that God could forgive him or her might hear the possibility of God's gracious acceptance.

Diversity

Sally in Chapter 1 also noted diversity in adult ability to deal with difficult material as well as in interests and life-styles.

With students who seem so far ahead that they should be teaching the class—rejoice! The notion that the teacher always has to know more than the students does not work too well with children and youth, and is positively ludicrous when teaching adults. Teaching adults in the church should not primarily be the communication of material by an expert with superior knowledge to students who have little knowledge (although occasionally that may happen). Rather, it is a matter of teacher (or, probably better, group leader) sharing together with group members in the exciting enterprise of discovering the depths of the Bible and the Christian faith and life. And theologically, this is the way it should be. All of us who are baptized share equally in the redeeming grace of

God. None of us is an expert on God—except in so far as we have received God's revelation to us all and have experienced his grace. And that makes all of us equally expert. The only human of whom this equality was not true was Jesus himself; he did indeed know more about the Father than we do. The Holy Spirit, Jesus' other self, is with us today, and it is the Spirit who is the expert teacher. All of us are mere learners. In teaching adults, it will be helpful to share this attitude verbally so that the class will feel free to explore ideas and will not be held back by politely trying to pretend that in everything you know more than anyone else present. When everyone shares their talents and insights, wonderfully enriching adult learning can take place. Adults have many insights from their own thinking, from experience, from reading, and from listening and conversing with others. These all become resources as adults share the good news. [28]

What about the diversity that Sally noted among adults' life-styles and interests? [29] There is a sense in which there is homo-geneity in any group dealing with the gospel—all are sinners and all need God's gracious acceptance and forgiveness in Christ. On the other hand, we have already mentioned the ways in which persons in different stages of adulthood may experience the question and may seek the answer in relation to their own situation. Give plenty of opportunity for discussion and allow time for personal thinking and reflection to help take account of this diversity. Booklists may also be a way to encourage learners to do additional independent reading in areas which particularly interest them.

Probably we need to consider seriously the importance of having several groups of adults all dealing with the same broad topic. They need not meet simultaneously. Given today's diverse schedules, they probably should meet at different times of the year and for lesser or greater periods, some on weekdays, some in evenings, and perhaps some in a retreat setting. And we should not be surprised if the make-up of the groups differ. People want to explore the implications of the gospel in many ways. They have differing experiences to feed into discussion. Not every adult finds every group 'just right' for them. Flexible scheduling and flexible approaches are required. And we should not be affronted if an adult says that he or she is interested in the topic we are addressing but would rather deal with it in a different way. Such comments are to be expected and respected. The helpful teacher will then seek to recommend a group or a book that may help the adult learner move in the direction he or she is seeking.

Chapter 8

GOSPEL-INFORMED PROCEDURES

The gospel can be taught in verbal and nonverbal ways in the classroom. If we say things with our lips and deny them with our actions, then our message will be confusing at best and blatant hypocrisy at worst. Moreover, the more we can reinforce what we teach, the more likely it is to be grasped by the students. Reinforcement can be through verbal and nonverbal means. How, then, can we operate in the classroom so that our actions and attitudes support the gospel message?

Structure and freedom

We must be careful to avoid both a "laissez-faire" attitude that allows the student to proceed without guidance and also the opposite attitude that would control the student by indoctrination. Narrative happily avoids both extremes, since it is structured yet allows the listener freedom of apprehension and interpretation. But there will be other procedures in the class session besides narrative. In these activities also we shall want to give structure yet allow the learner as much freedom of expression, searching, and experimentation as possible. Creative activities which balance the need for structure and freedom are most likely to encourage the student to express learnings without excessive direction and domination on the part of the teacher. So, we shall want to include as many creative activities as we can. Creative activities include writing original stories, poems, songs, prayers, and music; dramatization; craft activities; drawing; painting; making montages and collages; making and using puppets; completion of open-ended stories and plays; imagining oneself in the story; and so on. Such activities may be done by individuals or by groups. Interest centers will allow you to offer a wide choice of creative activities per lesson as well as helping you cope with the variety of interests and abilities that may be represented in the class members.

Creative activities also provide opportunities for learners to experience acceptance on the part of the teacher and peers—acceptance not of previously-determined answers or specific patterns of craft items but of the learner's own creations which arise out of his or her particular understandings, attitudes, and feelings, and therefore are closely related to the individual's self-concept. This acceptance can be a pointer toward, a reminder of, the unconditional acceptance we all need and which we receive in the gospel.

Whole-brain function and creativity

Current brain theory has shown that the left hemisphere of the brain is concerned with written and spoken language, logical reasoning, analytical skills, and mathematical abilities. The right hemisphere is concerned with the emotions, spatial construction and pattern sense, nonverbal ideation, perception of meaning, body scheme, certain aspects of our self-identity, creative insight, artistic and musical skills, and intuitive functions. (This pattern is typical for righthanded individuals. Left-handed persons sometimes show this pattern and sometimes show a reversal of the hemispheric functions.)[1]

Education—including religious education—has often tended to favor the left hemisphere processes. Theorists in the last decade have asked how it is possible to educate holistically, using both hemispheres.[2] One answer may lie in the creative process which has a transformational pattern.

Daniel Batson, writing on psychological dynamics of creativity, puts forward six propositions, which summarize one psychological interpretation of the creative process.[3] First, our reality is constructed. Second, the reality we construct is based on our cognitive structures. Third, these cognitive structures are hierarchically arranged so that specific dimensions are grouped under general organizing principles which are grouped in turn under more abstract organizing principles and so on. Fourth, creativity involves an improvement in one's cognitive organization toward greater differentiation and integration, that is, an increase in the number of organizing principles; such creative change transcends old ways of looking at the world. Fifth, there are identifiable stages in the creative process—incubation, illumination, and verification. Sixth, the creative sequence may have a physiological base with the preparation stage being handled by the logical left hemisphere, the incubation stage by the right hemisphere reorganizing the cognitive structures and thus leading to insight or illumination, and the verification returning to the left hemisphere for the logical testing of the insight.[4]

Batson shows that psychological therapy and many religious experiences show the pattern of the creative process—an experience of transformation or new vision or new life is often typical of the description given by individuals of such experiences.[5] Transformation in the cognitive structures results in such cases in new understandings of deeply existential questions. Rather than cold, calculated facts, "they are invested with great personal meaning and so are accompanied by strong emotions."[6] Batson rejects the analysis of religious experience that focuses mainly on emotional aspects. In his view, the change is one of creativity and cognitive structure, which lies so close to the individual's reality structure that the whole of the person is involved and so the transformation is accompanied by strong emotions.[7]

From Batson's theory we may draw several implications for teaching that will help us in communicating the gospel. First, narrative itself holds together the bifurcated reality of the separate functions of the brain hemispheres. On the one hand, narrative is logical and verbal. On the other hand, narrative calls forth the emotions and invites insightful responses. Thus, stories both make sense and are imaginative.[8] They put together our dualistic experience.

Transformational narrative is particularly able to facilitate the integration of the hemisphere functions since it is inherently creative. New insight, a new way of grasping reality is essential in transformation. In fact, the pattern of Batson's creative process (preparation, incubation, illumination, and verification) reflects the transformational pattern[9] which is present in transformational narrative. Therefore, it facilitates the integration of the hemisphere functions and fosters creativity. And, additional creative activities in the learning process in turn will support and facilitate the grasp of the transformational pattern.

We said that faith is a whole-person function. It is not solely intellectual or solely emotional or solely volitional, but includes all aspects of the person. If we are to present the gospel so that persons respond to the Word in faith, then religious education must be a whole-brain activity, an integrative activity of the mind, in which left and right hemispheres enhance and enrich each other, and, in the interplay, open the way for creative and transforming experience.

In teaching, then, you will want to increase the students' opportunity for creative activities that utilize both hemispheres of the brain. Not only hearing narratives, but writing stories, poetry, and songs, will be helpful. Allow for the students to use insight, music, and artistic skills, and to use intuitive skills. Minimize mere repetition of logical and factual material. Include creative activities and creative thinking in class that will foster the transformational pattern and so facilitate the grasp of transformational narrative. In teaching adults, you may find this particularly challenging. Many adults are so used to cognitive learning in religious education that they find themselves somewhat rusty on creative skills and may resist using them. However, with patience and persuasion, adults not only can be very creative but will enjoy such experiences thoroughly.

Bear in mind Batson's description of uncreative religious experiences as those which involve rigid adherence to a specific solution that emphasizes only one aspect of a problem and ignores others. Creative experiences take account of various aspects of the problem. Allow students the opportunity to think and explore options instead of presenting them with just one way to think and insisting that they adhere rigidly to it.

Acceptance of students

We have said in previous chapters that teacher and peer acceptance, though broken and conditional, can be prototype of the acceptance of which the gospel speaks. While always sinful, in the grasp of the Spirit the teacher must seek to accept students in such a way that they are led to recognize the need for unconditional acceptance. Your accepting relationship with students can be a pointer to God's acceptance, an analog of the gospel.[10] Paul Tillich suggests that *agape* should be the attitude of the Christian educator, showing acceptance of the one who deserves to be rejected even as God himself accepts us. Such an attitude is not possible without personal prayer and a willingness to learn of the gospel ourselves. We may, of course, expect that we shall learn as much of acceptance and forgiveness from our students as they will from us. In fact, your very acceptance of the students can be a factor in helping the students accept you in turn—and vice versa.[11]

If you have prior-to-class experiences (a problem at home, for example) that make warm relationships difficult, it will be helpful to verbalize this and ask for the students' understanding from the beginning of the class. Such sharing will prevent your behavior or worried facial expression from being misunderstood.

In addition to your own accepting attitude, students will receive peer acceptance as prototype of the gospel. Peer acceptance sometimes can be tricky to obtain without undue teacher dominance. Elementary children and early adolescents are particularly skilled in critiquing peers! And this, in spite of the fact that the concrete thinker is able to appreciate the point of view of others when helped to do so, and the abstract thinker most definitely has the capacity to see how remarks and actions will communicate acceptance and rejection of other students. Children can be notoriously cruel in putting down others by words, facial expressions, and actions. Some children still need help in recognizing when they have done so. Many need help in overcoming the "fairness" attitude of "he deserved it—anybody that says something that stupid deserves to be laughed at." And, it is not only children and early youth who need to be cautioned. Older youth and adults have more sophisticated ways of indicating rejection that are no less harmful and unkind. In the learning setting, we must endeavor to provide an atmosphere in which students can experience peer acceptance.

Peer acceptance may be particularly important in the case of students who have experienced unusual amounts of peer rejection. At the children's level these may be students who are mentally or physically impaired or who have disfigurements or are overweight. At the youth and adult level, they may be those who reflect society's oppression of persons of color, women, persons whose language is other than English, and the elderly, to name just a few. For children, it is sometimes helpful to establish "rules" or guidelines for behavior that is "accepting" as the series of lessons proceeds. For all ages, your modeling behavior will be crucial.

Participation

Keep in mind what we have said about participating in the students' situation in order to interpret the *question* and the *answer* in the most helpful ways. Listen carefully to the issues your students raise. Get to know their life-styles and concerns. While your own experience is valuable, it may not be similar to that of your students. So, before you share your own story, consider whether it really speaks to the students. Would another illustration work better because it more nearly depicts your students' situation? Similarly consider your terminology. Will it speak to the learners? Phrases that are dear to you may not necessarily be the best to use with your students. If so, retain your loved phrases for your own devotional use but seek new ones to communicate with the students.

Participation should be kept in mind when choosing input. For example, if you use Bible stories with children, be careful that the narratives do not come across as stories about what God does for grown-ups. Since the predicament of estrangement is the same for both adults and children, stories of Jesus and adults can be useful. But they must be structured so that the child identifies with the *question* and also with the way in which the *answer* is presented. Similarly, youth may find some Bible stories removed from their own situation. And adults also may feel that settings from the Bible or church history are far removed from modern times. Discussion following the reading of Bible passages or the telling of narratives will enable the students to explore their questions and identify with the *question* and *answer.* It will also show your respect for and acceptance of the students' efforts to wrestle with issues in their own way.

Atmosphere

The classroom appearance and atmosphere should suggest warmth and interest in your students. For children, a typical classroom may be a welcome and familiar setting. But they will appreciate appropriate pictures at their eye-level and furniture that enables their feet to touch the floor. These tell the children that you care about them. Acceptance will also be communicated by means of a colorful and cheerful well-lit room, set up in advance so that students feel welcomed and invited to participate from the moment they arrive.

Youth may feel more acceptance if you provide a special place just for them and allow them to decorate it as they wish. And adults may prefer someone's living room to a cold church building. Whatever helps students feel that you and the church care about them will contribute to your teaching of the gospel.

Discipline

In teaching children and youth, discipline is a prerequisite for any learning to take place. It is not really a procedure so much as a precondition for learning. The classroom experience of discipline should not contradict the spoken message of the gospel. The gospel is the message of God's gracious forgiveness and acceptance in spite of what we are: it includes the fact that God does not ignore what we are and have done, but accepts us despite the fact that we are unacceptable. The teacher, therefore, cannot ignore unacceptable behavior: it should be corrected gently but firmly with a reminder that the reason for discipline is so that all of the students are able to learn. But the teacher must avoid words and actions that suggest condemnation or that condone peer-condemnation. Warm, caring, and verbalized acceptance and forgiveness are appropriate if disturbing behavior occurs. Verbalization is important, especially in the elementary years. It is not until about ten years of age that forgiveness is understood in terms of restoring broken relationships (as opposed merely to letting the child off an expected punishment). Children from nine to twelve years are either just approaching this point or are just practicing the newfound art of forgiveness. Verbal reminders are helpful.

Avoid the temptation to overuse behavior problems as opportunities to "teach a point." If every small point of discipline becomes the focus of a sermon on forgiveness, the gospel message will be lost in public humiliation. Desirable is a personal one-to-one (or more, if the problem involves more than one child) verbal dealing with the situation in a quiet way that does not draw attention to the student(s) in question.

Worship

In the classroom we should not attempt to duplicate the ritual of the church service. However, in teaching justification there should be an important place for prayer, praise, and music. There are several reasons for this emphasis.

Prayer will give opportunity personally and corporately to ask for the forgiveness about which the class is learning. Prayer and singing will give opportunity to thank and praise God for his gracious forgiveness and acceptance.

Further, songs and devotional Bible passages will reinforce the message of justification.[12] Sometimes we are told that if we really want to know what people believe, just look at the hymns they sing! There is some truth to this. Singing is powerful personal reinforcement of a message. Major historical political and military campaigns have recognized the power of music in helping persons identify with the message for which they are standing or fighting. In selecting songs that reflect God's gracious acceptance, be sure to choose those suitable for the age-level. Hymns for congregational worship may be eminently suitable for adults and older youth, but you may need different songs to express grace for children and younger youth.

Including devotional experiences in the classroom will balance the lesson in favor of grace. There no doubt will be plenty of opportunity in sessions for students to express the *question* and to reflect on situations in which they have experienced guilt, or have felt that they have been condemned by God and/or people. It is equally important to allow for joyful thanksgiving so that sessions are not grim. Your aim is to teach God's gracious forgiveness, not to indulge in morbid self-examination. While the gospel cannot be heard without the law, nevertheless there must be no likelihood that students go away feeling that the law was more thoroughly examined than the good news. Joyful worship may be particularly appropriate in setting the right tone at the beginning of a session and in summing up at the end of the session.

For children, such prayer and praise can help in overcoming the difficulty children have in relating to Jesus in the present. Children conceive of God and Jesus concretely. Since the children relate each noun to a concrete referent with a spatial location, God and Jesus tend to be conceived as separate "people." Some teachers try vainly to explain the Trinity abstractly to children— an exercise in futility since the abstract reasoning is beyond the children's grasp. Other teachers attempt to reserve the term *Jesus* for the historical figure who lived two thousand years ago, while referring to divine being in the present as *God*. The latter approach can make it difficult for children to relate to Jesus as the one who can bring acceptance and new life for them. Few children will raise the issue themselves unless a well-meaning teacher attempts to explain the matter. It is probably better simply to assert God's love and forgiveness for people long ago and today alongside the love and forgiveness of Jesus as the Christ. Children may then make their own connection that the same love and forgiveness shown by God was and is precisely the same as that shown by Jesus. Instead of abstract reasoning about the relation of God and Jesus, the children may simply address praise and thanksgiving to Jesus as to God. Moreover, the children need opportunity to experience the presence of Jesus in the classroom. Class worship that includes confession, praise, and thanksgiving through prayer and song can fulfill this need.

Finally, it will be important to maintain a deep tie between what happens in the classroom and what happens in the congregational service of worship. Classroom devotions in no way replace the preaching of the Word and the proclamation of God's mercy and forgiveness in the Sacraments. The center of the students' response to God will inevitably be expressed in the midst of God's people as they confess, hear the Word, and rejoice together as the worshiping community. Children as well as youth and adults are enriched by experiencing the Christian symbols and receiving the gospel in worship. Certainly, children may not understand every word. But to praise and pray and celebrate God's redemption with the gathered community of believers is a powerful reinforcement of that which occurs in the classroom. This means that there is an inherent problem with situations that schedule Sunday church school at the same time as the worship service. To suggest that some age-levels (usually children) should appropriately learn, while others (usually adults) should worship totally negates true teaching of the gospel. Learners should be worshipers and vice versa, except perhaps for the youngest children for whom sitting in rows for an hour is very difficult. It is a serious error to prevent persons from having the opportunity to learn as well as worship by forcing them to choose between the two.

Theology and method

All that we have said in this chapter assumes that our theological concern—justification by grace through faith—has inevitable implications for classroom methodology. Some thinkers would argue that the "interference" of theology can only be detrimental in determining the objectives and methodology of religious education.[13] Others would contend that the content is primary and that methods are of little importance.[14] Still others say that action comes first, and reflection follows.[15] The approach that we have taken is that goals, methods, and procedures should arise directly from, and be reflective of, theology. To communicate the gospel, one needs verbalization and content, but also attitudes and behaviors that support and reinforce the verbalization.

Your own faith

Finally, there will be no greater support in teaching the gospel than your own joyous and thankful response to God's gracious forgiveness in Christ. Persons may, perhaps, teach some secular subjects without enjoying them. Their students' motivation will probably be low since it is almost impossible to hide one's lack of enjoyment in teaching. But, some learning will undoubtedly occur if the textbooks and methodology are good enough.

Not so with the gospel. A teacher who does not believe the good news can do no more than recite sterile phrases. We have said that faith is a whole-person response. Your students need to see your whole-person response to God's action in Christ, not only in your words but also in your attitudes, your behavior, your participation in worship, your enthusiasm in witnessing. This does not mean that you must put on a bubbly front. Students quickly sense the depth of quiet faith and the serenity in a life of prayer and meditation on the Scriptures.

Your own acceptance of God's prior acceptance of you in Jesus Christ can be a proclamation in itself. Your faith can act as a symbol. It can point beyond itself to the justification which it receives and the Christ who is the source of faith. In this way, you as teacher become part of the communication of the good news.

APPENDIX

Perhaps the easiest way to help you structure your own transformational narratives is to give you some examples of the pattern. The analyses may look strange at first, but they are simple to do.

Following are structural analyses of six Bible stories that communicate God's gracious acceptance in Jesus. The analyses follow the "model IV" schematic form of Maranda and Maranda.

You may recall that we described the pattern in general terms in Chapter 5. It is expressed technically as

$$f_x(a) \; : \; f_y(b) \; :: \; f_x(b) \; : \; f_a\text{-}l(y)$$

In this formula, the symbol or agent (a) seeks a solution through an inadequate means (f_x) but the attempts fail to provide a solution. Then symbol or agent (b) seeks a solution, but uses an adequate means or function (f_y) opposite to the inadequate attempts of (a). (b) thus participates in the function (a) set out to accomplish, (f_x), but does so in a way that reverses the situation for (a) and enables (a) to participate in the successful solution provided by (b). Not only does (a) participate in the successful function (f_y), but the final situation is a gain for (a).

The functional semantic mediating symbol is (b). (b) straddles both sides of the formula, doing what (a) attempted, but doing it in a way that is the opposite of (a), and so producing the successful outcome in which (a) shares. (b) thus accomplishes the "transformation."

In each analysis, the structure of the story is diagrammed schematically, with negative aspects on the left and positive aspects on the right. This scheme is then expressed as a diagram in which the final outcome (arrow) is always on the "positive" side, showing that the successful solution to the problem is a gain and not merely a reversal of the original situation. If you diagram your own stories, the pattern should look like this. If the pattern does not come out with a diagram of this shape, then you probably are dealing with a story that has an inherently different structure.

The diagrammed pattern is followed by an analysis as a formula that is explained by the "reading" that follows. Maranda and Maranda also use a cause-effect framework to express the result of the first agent's function and the opposite result of the second agent's function (QS : QR :: FS : FR). This analysis is also followed by a "reading."

Either analysis will help you in checking your story structure. The analyses are quick ways to get the transformational structure clearly in mind so that you can tell the story in a way that emphasizes the main point of Jesus' acceptance. Again, if you find or create a story that just does not seem to fit the formulae, you probably have a story that does not reflect the transformational pattern. This does not mean it is not a good story; it just means that you might want to use it for a purpose other than that suggested for transformational narrative in Chapter 5.

Zacchaeus

The story of Zacchaeus (Luke 19:1-9) may be analyzed structurally as follows:

—	+
Zacchaeus collects taxes and more People hate Zacchaeus	
	Zacchaeus wants to see Jesus Zacchaeus climbs a tree Jesus tells Zacchaeus he is coming to his house Zacchaeus receives Jesus joyfully
People complain at Jesus' acceptance of Zacchaeus	
	Zacchaeus gives half of his goods to the poor and restores fourfold the money he has taken wrongfully Jesus declares that salvation has come to Zacchaeus's household

That is:

As a figure:

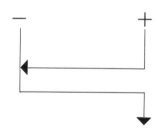

As a formula:

    Terms:
        a - Zacchaeus
        b - Jesus
    Functions:
        x - being acceptable
        y - being unacceptable
        $f_x(a) : f_y(b) :: f_x(b) : f_a\text{-}1(y)$

Reading: Zacchaeus is in a double bind situation. On the one hand, he finds his life-style acceptable as he profits from taking inflated taxes. And this life-style results in his being unacceptable to the populace. Therefore, on the other hand, perhaps deep down he is less than satisfied with himself—at all events, he wants to see Jesus. Jesus, the Acceptable One, becomes unacceptable to the people as he identifies with unacceptable Zacchaeus in offering friendship to him. (The One who will ultimately identify with the unacceptable human race on the cross already prefigures in his life that identification with the unacceptable.) Jesus' acceptance of Zacchaeus in spite of his unacceptableness results in the permutation of Zacchaeus's self-acceptance. He now finds his old life unacceptable (as shown in his turning over his life-style and giving back the money). Zacchaeus now accepts his new self which is rooted in Jesus' acceptance of him.

In the terms of structural analysis, Jesus is the agent or "semantic mediator" who solves the problem and produces a new and better situation.

In the cause-effect framework:

QS: Self-centered Zacchaeus taking taxes and also additional money wrongfully

QR: Estrangement from other people, God, and himself

FS: Jesus' acceptance of Zacchaeus

FR: Zacchaeus's change of life-style—victory over estrangement through Jesus' acceptance; new being for Zacchaeus

$$QS : QR :: FS : FR$$

Reading: If Zacchaeus's self-centered accumulation of riches results in estrangement from others and from the person he ought to be, then Jesus' acceptance of Zacchaeus results in a new other-centered life-style in which acceptance by himself and others is rooted in the new being in Jesus as the Christ.

The forgiven woman

Following is an analysis of the story of the Forgiven Woman (Luke 7:36-50).

−	+
The woman is a sinner The woman is despised by others	

	Jesus tells the woman she
	  is forgiven
	The woman approaches Jesus
	  at Simon's house
	The woman anoints Jesus'
	  feet

Simon criticizes Jesus and the woman	

	Jesus reaffirms the
	  woman's forgiveness
	The onlookers are amazed
	Jesus relates the woman's
	  faith to her salvation

That is:

−	+
− −	
	+ + +
−	
	+ + +

As a figure:

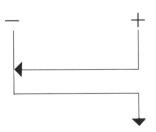

As a formula:

Terms:

    a - Woman

    b - Jesus

Functions:

    x - being acceptable

    y - being unacceptable

    $f_x(a) : f_y(b) :: f_x(b) : f_a\text{-}1(y)$

Reading: The woman is in a typical double bind situation. She sees herself as acceptable, yet also unacceptable, in her life-style that reflects alienation from God and from people. Her acceptance of that alien life-style results in her being unacceptable to the populace. The One who will be crucified prefigures the Cross in his identification with the woman. In this identification, Jesus becomes unacceptable to the onlookers as he receives the woman's gestures of love and gratitude. (Simon the Pharisee represents the onlookers' attitude to both Jesus and the woman.) But Jesus' acceptance of the woman in spite of her unacceptableness results in the permutation of her self-acceptance. She repents and responds to Jesus with love and faith. Her whole-hearted love and faith in God's grace are rooted in Jesus' acceptance of her in pronouncing forgiveness. In the process, Jesus declares Simon's attitude to be unacceptable.

In the transformational structure, Jesus is the agent or "semantic mediator" who solves the problem and produces a new and better situation. It is through him that the transformation occurs.

In the cause-effect framework:

QS: The woman living a sinful life

QR: Estrangement from people and from God

FS: Jesus' acceptance of the woman in pronouncing forgiveness

FR: Reconciliation with God, victory over estrangement and a new life of devotion, thanksgiving, and faith for the woman

$$QS : QR :: FS : FR$$

Reading: If the woman's sinfulness leads to estrangement from people and from God, then Jesus' acceptance of the woman in pronouncing forgiveness leads to reconciliation with God, victory over estrangement and a new life of faith and love.

Peter's denial and restoration

The story of Peter's denial and restoration (John 13:36-38; 18:15-18, 25-27; and 21:15-19) may be analyzed as follows:

—	+
	Peter promises to remain loyal
Jesus predicts the denial	
Jesus is arrested	
	Peter and a disciple follow to the courtyard
Peter denies Jesus	
	Peter and the disciples net a great catch
	Jesus gives Peter the chance to affirm his love three times
	Peter becomes a great preacher and loyal follower of Jesus

That is:

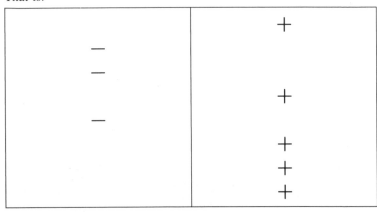

As a figure:

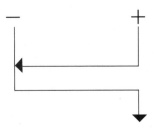

As a formula:

Terms:

a - Peter

b - Jesus

Functions:

x - being loyal and loving

y - receiving disloyalty and unlove

$$f_x(a) : f_y(b) :: f_x(b) : f_a\text{-}l(y)$$

Reading: Peter's loyalty to and love of self result in his being disloyal and unloving to Jesus. But Jesus' loyalty to and love of Peter in spite of his disloyalty results in the permutation of self-love, reorienting Peter in new and more permanent loyalty and love to his Lord.

Thus Jesus is the semantic mediator in the story who solves the initial problem and produces a new and better situation.

In the cause-effect frame:

    QS: Peter being disloyal and unloving
    QR: Estrangement from Jesus
    FS: Jesus being loyal and loving
    FR: Jesus, crucified and risen, healing estrangement and restoring Peter to loyalty and love

$$QS : QR :: FS : FR$$

Reading: If Peter's disloyalty and unlove result in estrangement, then Jesus' ultimate loyalty and love (exemplified in the Cross where he receives total unlove and rejection yet loves to the end) lead to the victory over estrangement and to new being for Peter.

The story of Paul

The narrative of Paul (Acts 26:9-18; Romans 3:21-26) can be analyzed as follows:

—	+
	Saul wants to please God
But he keeps doing those things he knows he should not do	
Saul persecutes the Christians	
	Jesus confronts Saul on the Damascus road
Saul wonders who it is	
	Jesus identifies himself
	Jesus tells Paul he will be a witness to the Gentiles
	Paul understands the gospel of forgiveness by grace through faith
	Paul preaches and writes letters about Jesus

That is:

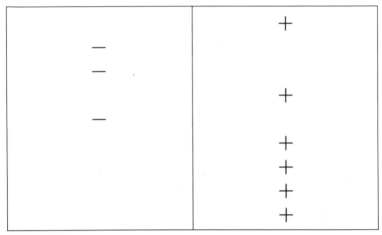

As a figure:

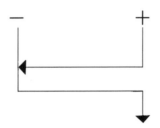

As a formula:

The Acts passage and the Romans passage both lend themselves to the chiasmic structure of transformational narrative. Therefore, two analyses will follow.

On the basis of Romans 3:21-26:
Terms:
a - Saul
b - Jesus

Appendix

Function:
    x - attempting to overcome sin
    y - being overcome by sin
    $f_x(a) : f_y(b) :: f_x(b) : f_a\text{-}1(y)$

Reading: Saul attempts to overcome sin by works of the law. But, the more he tries to fulfill the law, the more he experiences being overcome by sin and being condemned by the law. Jesus takes on himself the negativities of estrangement and sin on the Cross and triumphs over them. Therefore, Jesus' attempt to overcome sin is truly efficacious. And Paul by faith shares in that victory and is freed from having to earn God's favor which he now realizes is received as gift.

    Jesus is the One through whom the answer to the human situation is given.

On the basis of Acts 26:9-18:
    Terms:
        a - Saul
        b - Jesus
    Function:
        x - hating
        y - loving
        $f_x(a) : f_y(b) :: f_x(b) : f_a\text{-}1(y)$

Reading: Saul's efforts lead to hating and persecuting the Christians. Jesus is always loving; but Jesus takes on himself Paul's hatred in persecuting his followers (even as he took on himself the hatred and estrangement and sin of the world as the Crucified One). And so Paul's estrangement is overcome, his hatred ceases and he is enabled to love and to serve the Lord whom he previously persecuted.

    Again, Jesus is the One through whom the initial problem is solved (the "semantic mediator" of the structural analysis, through which a new and better situation comes into being).

In the cause-effect frame:
    QS: Paul is unable to get right with God by himself
    QR: Paul's persecution of the Christians who preach the gospel of
        love and forgiveness through Jesus

FS: Jesus grasps Paul in love and forgiveness
FR: Paul responds in faith and becomes a preacher of the gospel
of love and forgiveness through Jesus

QS : QR :: FS : FR

Reading: If Paul's attempts to get right with God by means of the law result in frustration and rejection of grace in the gospel of Jesus the Christ, then Jesus' initiative in grasping Paul and offering forgiveness by grace results in Paul's response of faith that receives grace and goes on to preach to others about grace through Jesus the Christ.

The Emmaus event

The story of the disciples on the road to Emmaus (Luke 24:13-35) can be analyzed as follows:

—	+
The disciples are sad— Jesus has died and their hopes are dashed	
	Jesus meets the disciples on the way to Emmaus
The disciples do not recognize Jesus	
	Jesus explains the Scriptures about himself
Jesus acts as if going on	
	The disciples invite Jesus to stay
	Jesus breaks the bread
	The disciples recognize him
	The disciples go back to tell the eleven

That is:

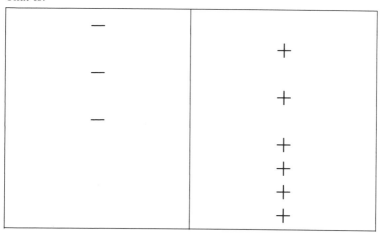

As a figure:

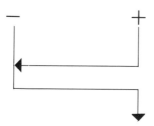

As a formula:
Terms:
a - disciples
b - Jesus
Function:
x - having false hope
y - having true hope
$f_x(a) : f_y(b) :: f_x(b) : f_a\text{-}1(y)$

Reading: The disciples are shattered because they have been falsely hoping for the restoration of Israel and a messiahship rooted in nationalistic expectations. Jesus, who in himself is true hope, joins the disciples and listens to their disillusionment. He receives their false hopes and exposes them for what they are. In the encounter, Jesus reveals himself as the One who has and provides true hope beyond the restoration of Israel, as the Resurrected One who will continue to be their hope whether or not the disciples can see him and who will be with them in the breaking of the bread to renew true hope.[1]

Again, the agent in the analysis that enables the transformation is Jesus.

In the cause-effect frame:

QS: The disciples do not believe that Jesus has risen

QR: The disciples' false hopes are shattered; they return to Emmaus, puzzled and disillusioned

FS: Jesus reveals to the disciples his risen presence and brings true hope

FR: The disciples rush joyfully to tell their faith to others

$$QS : QR :: FS : FR$$

Reading: If the disciples' false hopes and disbelief in the Resurrection lead to disillusionment and despair, then Jesus' presence that brings true hope results in faith and joyful sharing of the news of hope in Jesus.

Doubting Thomas

The story of Thomas (John 20:24-29) may be analyzed structurally as follows:

—	+
Thomas refuses to believe without hard evidence	The disciples tell Thomas that Jesus has risen Jesus appears to Thomas and offers himself as evidence Thomas believes Jesus commends those who believe without the evidence of sight

That is:

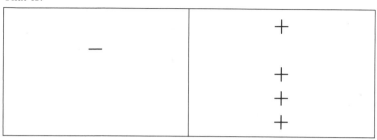

As a figure:

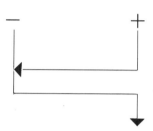

As a formula:

Terms:

a - Thomas

b - Jesus

Function:

x - having evidence

y - not having evidence

$$f_x(a) : f_y(b) :: f_x(b) : f_a\text{-}1(y)$$

Reading: Thomas has evidence that Jesus has been crucified and thus rejects the evidence (of the disciples' witness) that Jesus is alive. But Jesus appears as the evidence of his own victory and Thomas accepts this evidence without question, thus faith replaces doubt.

Again, Jesus is the semantic mediator in the narrative who solves the initial problem in the story and produces a new and better situation.

Or, in the cause-effect frame:

QS: Thomas believes that Jesus is dead and defeated

QR: Thomas refuses the disciples' witness to the Resurrection—
    he doubts the Lord and his victory

FS: Jesus appears to Thomas as the evidence of his own Lordship
    and victory

FR: Thomas believes in Jesus as Lord and God

$$QS : QR :: FS : FR$$

Reading: If Thomas's insistence on evidence leads him to doubt the victory of his Lord's resurrection, then Jesus' appearance as the evidence of who he is results in Thomas's unquestioning belief and commitment to his risen Lord.

NOTES

Quotations from the Lutheran Confessions are from the *Book of Concord,* trans. and ed. Theodore G. Tappert (Philadelphia: Fortress Press, 1959), and are abbreviated as follows:

BC, AC   The Augsburg Confession
BC, Apol. Apology of the Augsburg Confession
BC, SA   The Smalcald Articles
BC, SC   The Small Catechism
BC, LC   The Large Catechism
BC, Epit.   Formula of Concord, Epitome
BC, SD   Formula of Concord, Solid Declaration

Chapter 1

1. James F. Anderson, *Paul Tillich* (Albany, N.Y.: Magi Books, 1972), p. 4.
2. Paul Tillich, *Dynamics of Faith* (New York: Harper and Brothers, 1957), pp. 30-40.
3. Ibid., pp. 30-31.
4. David Elkind, *Children and Adolescents: Interpretive Essays on Jean Piaget,* 3d ed. (New York: Oxford University Press, 1981), p. 22. It is important to note that although the stages are related to, they are not determined by, age. See David Elkind, *Child Development and Education: A Piagetian Perspective* (New York: Oxford University Press, 1976), p. 84.
5. Ved P. Varma and Phillip Williams, *Piaget, Psychology and Education* (Itasca, Ill.: F. E. Peacock Publishers, 1976), p. 31.

6. See Jean Piaget, *Six Psychological Studies,* trans. Anita Tenzer (London: University of London Press, 1968), pp. 8-70.

7. For an excellent summary of the characteristics of the sensory-motor period, see John H. Flavell, *The Developmental Psychology of Jean Piaget* (New York: D. Van Nostrand Co., 1963), Chapter 3.

8. During the concrete stage the child comes to use operations based on the grouping structure—class inclusion operations and serial ordering operations. See translator's introduction to Barbel Inhelder and Jean Piaget, *Growth of Logical Thinking from Childhood to Adolescence,* trans. Anne Parsons and Stanley Milgram (New York: Basic Books, 1958), pp. *xv-xvi.* Concrete operations are described in detail in Jean Piaget and Barbel Inhelder, *The Psychology of the Child,* trans. Helen Weaver (New York: Basic Books, 1969), Chapter 4. Also, on concrete operations see Flavell, *Developmental Psychology,* Chapter 5; and Dorothy G. Singer and Tracey A. Revenson, *A Piaget Primer: How a Child Thinks* (New York: New America Library, Times Mirror, 1978), pp. 20-24.

9. On the three mental processes which guide the concrete child's thinking—negation, reciprocation, and identity—see Ruth L. Ault, *Children's Cognitive Development: Piaget's Theory and the Process Approach* (New York: Oxford University Press, 1977), p. 63.

10. See Piaget's works, *The Child's Conception of Movement and Speed, The Child's Conception of Time, The Child's Conception of Space* in Howard E. Gruber and J. Jacques Vonèche, eds., *The Essential Piaget* (New York: Basic Books, 1977), pp. 518-642.

11. See Piaget, *Six Psychological Studies,* pp. 62-64. For the difference between concrete and formal structures of thinking, see Inhelder and Piaget, *The Growth of Logical Thinking,* Chapter 17.

12. Some researchers, in fact, have suggested further refinements or sub-stages in adulthood. See Michael L. Commons, Francis A. Richards, and Deanna Kuhn, "Systematic and Metasystematic Reasoning: A Case for Levels of Reasoning beyond Piaget's Stage of Formal Operations," *Child Development* 53 (August 1982):1058-1069.

13. Lawrence Kohlberg posits three levels of moral development, each of which consists of two stages—a total of six stages altogether. The first three of Kohlberg's stages correspond to Piaget's preoperational, concrete, and abstract thinking stages while stages four, five, and six are found only in adults (although not in all adults). See Lawrence Kohlberg, *Essays on Moral Development,* vol. 1, *The Philosophy of Moral Development: Moral Stages and the Idea of Justice* (San Francisco: Harper and Row, 1981), Appendix A, "The Six Stages of Moral Judgment."

14. Ronald Goldman's research on religious conceptual development in English schoolchildren is detailed in his book, *Religious Thinking from Childhood to Adolescence* (New York: Seabury Press, 1964.) His recommendations

for curriculum are in his work, *Readiness for Religion: A Basis for Developmental Religious Education* (New York: Seabury Press, paperback ed., 1970.)

15. Goldman, *Religious Thinking*, p. 62.
16. Ibid., p. 89.
17. Ibid., pp. 90-91.
18. Ibid., p. 92. In addition to concepts of God, Goldman also describes in detail the development of a number of other religious concepts.
19. Ibid., p. 64. Goldman attributes the delay in appearance of religious formal operations to two possible factors—first, that religious thinking depends on general life experience and practice in general abstract thinking after the age of 11-plus, and second, the confusion in children's minds about religious matters due to poor or premature teaching.
20. Goldman, *Readiness*, pp. 42-43.
21. Goldman, *Religious Thinking*, pp. 222-223.
22. James W. Fowler, *Stages of Faith: The Psychology of Human Development and the Quest for Meaning* (San Francisco: Harper and Row, 1981), p. 133.
23. Ibid., p. 149.

Chapter 2

1. Paul Tillich, *Systematic Theology* (Welwyn, Hertfordshire, England: James Nisbet and Co., 1953), 1:71.
2. Ibid., p. 72.
3. Ibid.
4. Ibid., pp. 39-46.
5. Ibid., p. 52.
6. Ibid., pp. 55-56.
7. John P. Clayton (*The Concept of Correlation: Paul Tillich and the Possibility of a Mediating Theology* [Berlin, New York: Walter de Gruyter, 1980] p. 15) may well be correct in agreeing with Kenneth Hamilton, Walter Scharlemann, and Joachim Track, that Tillich's theological methodology cannot be reduced to the method of correlation alone. Nevertheless, it is the principal method of Tillich's *Systematic Theology* which is divided into five questions with correlated answers. Each question in some way reflects the broken, sinful, distorted state of our human existence—the conflicts of reason; finitude; estrangement from God, ourselves, and others; the ambiguities of life; and the ambiguities of history. To these questions, Tillich correlates the good news of God—the answers respectively of revelation; the being of God; New Being in Jesus as the Christ; the Spirit; and the kingdom of God.
8. On the points in this paragraph, see BC, SD V; BC, Apol. IV, 40, 57, 62, 257 and XII 34, 45, 52, 73, and 76, etc.
9. The author is indebted to the insights of Wayne G. Johnson, "Martin Luther's Law-Gospel Distinction and Paul Tillich's Method of Correlation: A

Study in Parallels," *Lutheran Quarterly* 23 (1971):274-288, and Wayne G. Johnson, *Theological Method in Luther and Tillich: Law-Gospel and Correlation* (Washington: University Press of America, 1981).

10. See John Macquarrie, *An Existentialist Theology: A Comparison of Heidegger and Bultmann* (London: S.C.M. Press, 1955), pp. 14, 199-200. Also, Rudolph Bultmann, *Jesus Christ and Mythology* (London: S.C.M. Press, 1960), pp. 52-53.

11. Gerhard Ebeling, "Existence Between God and God," *Journal for Theology and Church,* V (1968):150.

12. Tracy sees a correlation pattern in many contemporary writers such as Leslie Dewart, Gregory Baum, Langdon Gilkey, Van Harvey, and Gordon Kaufman.

13. David Tracy, *Blessed Rage for Order: The New Pluralism in Theology* (New York: Seabury Press, 1975), p. 34.

14. Ibid., pp. 45-6.

15. See, for example, Paul Tillich, *Theology of Culture,* ed. Robert C. Kimball (New York: Oxford University Press, Galaxy Book, 1964), Chapter 15.

16. Tillich, *Systematic Theology,* 3:207.

17. Ibid.

18. Tillich's statement, "The problem of religious education has become one of the major issues in the contemporary churches" (Ibid.), is still true. We can note his added claim that "the question of the meaning of the religious function of education has great importance for systematic theology." (Ibid.)

19. Tillich, *Theology of Culture,* p. 155.

20. Ibid., p. 156.

21. Tillich, *Systematic Theology,* 3:91.

22. Ibid., p. 107. See also, Paul Tillich, *The Protestant Era,* trans. J. L. Adams (Chicago: University of Chicago Press, abridged ed., 1957), p. 65; and Tillich, *Theology of Culture,* p. 153.

23. Tillich, *Theology of Culture,* p. 154.

24. Ibid., p. 155.

25. Tillich, *Systematic Theology,* 3:79-81.

26. Ibid., p. 80.

27. Ibid., p. 226. See also, Tillich, *The Religious Situation,* trans. H. R. Niebuhr (New York: Meridian Books, Living Age ed., 1956), pp. 146-149, on the relation between pupils and teacher.

28. Tillich, *Systematic Theology,* 3:207.

29. Tillich, *Theology of Culture,* pp. 204-205.

30. "We cannot use evidence to tell people that human nature is like it is. We can do it only in terms of risk." Ibid., p. 205.

31. Ibid., pp. 205-206.

32. Cf. ibid., p. 204.

33. Ibid., p. 154.

Notes

Chapter 3

1. BC, Apol. IV, 2, p. 107.
2. Eric W. Gritsch and Robert W. Jenson, *Lutheranism: The Theological Movement and Its Confessional Writings* (Philadelphia: Fortress Press, 1976), p. 36.
3. BC, Apol. IV, 2; BC, SD III, 6, 25. See also contemporary scholars such as Carl E. Braaten, *Principles of Lutheran Theology* (Philadelphia: Fortress Press, 1983), p. 34; Gerhard O. Forde, *Justification by Faith—A Matter of Death and Life* (Philadelphia: Fortress Press, 1982), p. 21; and Gritsch and Jenson, *Lutheranism,* p. 36.
4. See, for example, Harding Meyer and Lukas Vischer, eds., *Growth in Agreement: Reports and Agreed Statements of Ecumenical Conversations on a World Level* (New York: Paulist Press, 1984), pp. 174-175, 243, 250, 370-371. Also, H. George Anderson, T. Austin Murphy, and Joseph A. Burgess, *Justification by Faith: Lutherans and Catholics in Dialogue VII* (Minneapolis: Augsburg Publishing House, 1985).
5. BC, AC II, 1-14; BC, Apol. IV, 75.
6. BC, Apol. II, 3; IV, 33.
7. BC, SD I, 5, 6, 11.
8. BC, AC II, 2; BC, Apol. II, 35, 128.
9. BC, Apol. II, 14, 25-26.
10. BC, Epit. I, 2; BC, Apol. II, 18.
11. BC, SD I, 51.
12. Tillich, *Systematic Theology,* 1:52.
13. Ibid., p. 53. Neville A.C. Heuer (*Interpretative Theological Dynamics* [Durban: University of Durban-Westville, 1979], p. 85) notes that Tillich uses the Augsburg Confession definition of sin.
14. Tillich, *Systematic Theology,* 1:55. Also, on sin as un-love and un-faith in Luther, see Paul Tillich, *A History of Christian Thought,* ed. Carl E. Braaten (London: S.C.M. Press, 1968), p. 246.
15. BC, LC I, 22-23.
16. BC, SD III, 15, 55.
17. BC, SD III, 16; BC, AC XX, 28.
18. BC, SD III, 13.
19. Tillich, *Theology of Culture,* p. 209.
20. Tillich, *Systematic Theology,* 1:155.
21. BC, Apol. IV, 102, 116, 161, 165, 268, 307. Cf. Latin.
22. Paul Tillich, *The New Being* (New York: Charles Scribner's Sons, 1955), p. 12.
23. George Lindbeck supports the view that Tillich's understanding of justification is reflective of the Lutheran Confessions, and that Tillich's expansion of justification does not contradict the view of the Reformers. See his excellent article, "An Assessment Reassessed: Paul Tillich on the Reformation," *Journal of Religion* 63:4 (October 1983): 376-393.

24. Paul Tillich, *The Protestant Era,* trans. J. L. Adams (Chicago: University of Chicago Press, abridged ed., 1957), pp. 202-203.
25. Edmund Schlink, *Theology of the Lutheran Confessions,* trans. Paul F. Koehneke and Herbert J. A. Bouman (Philadelphia: Fortress Press, 1961), p. 82.
26. BC, LC II, 27-31. On Luther's view that Christology is basically soteriology, see Paul Althaus, *The Theology of Martin Luther,* trans. Robert C. Schultz (Philadelphia: Fortress Press, 1966), pp. 189, 192, 197, 230.
27. BC, SC II, 4.
28. BC, SD III, 56. Also, BC, AC III, 1-2, and BC, SD VIII, 87.
29. BC, SD VIII, 78. See also, BC, SD VIII, 76-84; BC, Apol. IV, 210; XXIV, 49, 90; BC, LC V, 22; BC, SD VII, 53, 61-62.
30. On faith as acceptance, see BC, Apol. IV, 46, 50, 53, 55, 56, 70, 84, 113, 155, 227, 264, 272, 285, 292, 297; BC, SD III, 25, 31, 38, 39, etc.
31. Wayne Mahan recognizes that Tillich's understanding of justification is precisely "the in-spite-of aspect of faith depicted classically by Luther's *'simil peccator, simul justus.'* " (Wayne W. Mahan, Tillich's System [San Antonio, Texas: Trinity University Press, 1974], p. 39.)
32. Tillich, *Systematic Theology* 2:53, 116, 179.
33. Tillich, *Theology of Culture,* p. 201.
34. Ibid., p. 155.
35. Fowler, *Stages,* p. 5.
36. See ibid., pp. 98ff.
37. Ibid., p. 99.
38. Fowler says, "In the domain of faith the assertion that more developed stages are in significant ways more adequate than less developed ones has to be made with even greater cautions and qualifications than in the cognitive or moral reasoning spheres. *Yet we cannot (and will not) avoid making and trying to corroborate that claim.* (Fowler, *Stages,* p. 101. My italics.)
39. Tillich explicitly repudiates the idea of quantitative progression in faith. If one is united to God in faith then one "is near God completely and absolutely." (Tillich, *History of Thought,* pp. 229-230.)
40. Goldman, *Readiness,* p. 192.
41. Tillich believes that this is possible on the basis of the *analogia entis:* because our being is related to God's being we can apply words about that which we know (for example, love) to God (Tillich, *Systematic Theology,* 1:266). See also, ibid., p. 264, and Tillich, *Love, Power and Justice: Ontological Analyses and Ethical Implications* (New York: Oxford University Press, 1960), pp. 109-110.
42. Tillich, *Dynamics,* pp. 49, 53.
43. David H. Kelsey, *The Fabric of Paul Tillich's Theology* (New Haven and London: Yale University Press, 1967), p. 48.
44. Ibid., p. 137.

Notes

Chapter 4

1. Fowler's term. See *Stages,* pp. 137, 149.
2. Margaret Anne Krych, "Communicating 'Justification' to Elementary-Age Children: A Study in Tillich's Correlational Method and Transformational Narrative for Christian Education," Ph.D. dissertation, Princeton Theological Seminary, June 1985, Part IV.
3. For example, Ronald Goldman, *Religious Thinking,* pp. 140-148, suggests that throughout the concrete stage the child moves from the concept of God as arbitrarily vengeful and punishing to that of God who punishes according to degrees of guilt. But it is not until at least 13 years of age that the child grasps that all humans are evil to some degree and even later that the child grasps God's love for sinners.
4. Tillich, *Theology of Culture,* p. 154.
5. Sigmund Freud, *The Basic Writings of Sigmund Freud,* trans. and ed. Dr. A. A. Brill (New York: Random House, The Modern Library, 1938), pp. 569-571, and also Sigmund Freud, *Collected Papers,* trans. Joan Riviere, 4 vols. (New York: Basic Books, 1959), 2:259-262. See also Erich Fromm, *The Anatomy of Human Destructiveness* (New York: Holt, Rinehart, and Winston, 1973), p. 218.
6. Richard A. Gardiner, *Therapeutic Communication with Children: The Mutual Storytelling Technique* (New York: Science House, 1971), p. 181.
7. Several themes of children's stories typify the *question.* Among them are violence, aggression, sibling rivalry, death, and hurt. Gardiner summarizes the findings of Ames and of Pitcher and Prelinger in ibid., pp. 180-181.
8. Paul Tillich, *Ultimate Concern: Tillich in Dialogue,* ed. D. Mackenzie Brown (London: S.C.M. Press, 1965), p. 120.
9. Ibid., p. 120-121.
10. David Elkind, *A Sympathetic Understanding of the Child: Birth to Sixteen* (Boston: Allyn and Bacon, 1974), p. 71.
11. Ibid., p. 68.
12. Ibid., p. 76.
13. Ibid., p. 88.
14. Paul Henry Mussen; John Janeway Conger; and Jerome Kagan, *Child Development and Personality,* 4th ed. (New York: Harper and Row, 1974), p. 425.
15. See ibid., pp. 429-431.
16. Ibid., p. 521.
17. Elkind, *Sympathetic Understanding,* p. 74.
18. Robert Kegan, *The Evolving Self* (Cambridge, Mass.: Harvard University Press, 1982), p. 165.
19. Elkind, *Sympathetic Understanding,* p. 69.
20. Mussen et al, *Child Development,* pp. 522-523.
21. Kegan, *The Evolving Self,* pp. 29, 33.
22. Ibid., Chapters 5, 6, 7.

23. Robert Kegan, "There the Dance Is: Religious Dimensions of a Developmental Framework" in Christiane Brusselmans et al., *Toward Moral and Religious Maturity* (The First International Conference on Moral and Religious Development, Morristown, N.J.: Silver Burdett Co., 1980), p. 421.

24. Kegan, *The Evolving Self,* p. 169.

25. Ibid., p. 170.

26. Kegan, "There the Dance Is," pp. 421-424.

27. Ibid., p. 161.

28. What Tillich analyzes as *hubris* and concupiscence.

29. Kegan, "There the Dance Is," p. 421.

30. Ibid., p. 414.

31. Tillich, *Systematic Theology,* 3:36-37.

32. Ibid., 1:271.

33. Ibid., 3:276.

34. James E. Loder, *The Transforming Moment: Understanding Convictional Experiences* (San Francisco: Harper and Row, 1981), p. 128.

35. Elkind, *Children and Adolescents,* p. 97.

36. On elementary children's views of death, see Edward White, Bill Elsom, and Richard Prawat, "Children's Conceptions of Death," *Child Development* 49:2 (June 1978): 307-310.

37. Ibid., p. 309.

38. Lawrence Kohlberg, *Essays on Moral Development* Vol. 1. *The Philosophy of Moral Development: Moral Stages and the Idea of Justice* (San Francisco: Harper and Row, 1981), pp. 340-341. Also see Goldman, *Religious Thinking,* pp. 136-137.

39. Dorothy H. Cohen, *The Learning Child* (New York: Random House, Pantheon Books, 1972), pp. 214, 275.

40. See Fowler, *Stages,* p. 150.

41. Krych, Dissertation, Part IV.

42. Althaus, *Theology of Martin Luther,* pp. 18-19.

43. Krych, Dissertation, Part IV.

Chapter 5

1. Fowler, *Stages,* p. 136. Also p. 149.

2. Gardiner, *Therapeutic Communication,* pp. 25-28.

3. Ibid., p. 68.

4. On structuralism see Edmund Leach, *Claude Lévi-Strauss* (New York: The Viking Press, 1970) and Jean Piaget, *Structuralism,* trans. and ed. Chaninah Maschler (New York: Harper and Row, 1970).

5. See, for example, the works of Claude Lévi-Strauss, including *Myth and Meaning* (New York: Schocken Books, 1979); *The Savage Mind* (Chicago: University of Chicago Press, 1966); *Race and History* (Paris: UNESCO, 1952); and *Structural Anthropology,* trans. Claire Jacobson and Brooke Grundfest Schoepf (Garden City, N.Y.: Doubleday and Co., Anchor Books

Notes

ed., 1967.) Helpful also is James A. Boon, *From Symbolism to Structuralism: Lévi-Strauss in a Literary Tradition* (New York: Harper and Row, 1972).

6. Elli Köngäs Maranda and Pierre Maranda, *Structural Models in Folklore and Transformational Essays*, Approaches to Semiotics No. 10, ed. Thomas A. Sebeok (The Hague, Paris: Mouton, 1971), pp. 21-22.
7. See ibid., pp. 25-36, 52-55, etc.
8. Ibid., pp. 83-86.
9. Loder, *Transforming Moment*, p. 132.
10. Krych, Dissertation, Part IV.
11. Loder, *Transforming Moment*, pp. 128-131. Also see James E. Loder, "Negation and Transformation: A Study in Theology and Human Development" in Christiane Brusselmans et al., *Toward Moral and Religious Maturity*, pp. 166-190.
12. Loder, *Transforming Moment*, p. 131.
13. Ibid., p. 31.
14. Ibid., p. 32.
15. Ibid., p. 32-33.
16. Ibid., p. 36.
17. Ibid., p. 33.
18. Ibid., p. 34.
19. Ibid., p. 61.
20. Ibid., p. 83.
21. Loder has a moving analysis of the Emmaus story in terms of the transformational pattern in ibid., pp. 96ff.
22. Tillich, *Systematic Theology,* 2:170, 174, 182-184.
23. In this sense we may agree with those who hold that "the potency of narrative structure and flow themselves are . . . the way of communicating the faith" (Gabriel Fackre, "Narrative Theology: An Overview," *Interpretation* 37:4 [October 1983]: 349).
24. Loder, *Transforming Moment,* p. 104.
25. Krych, Dissertation, Part IV.
26. Cf. the work of John Dominic Crossan, *The Dark Interval: Towards a Theology of Story* (Niles, Ill.: Argus Communications, 1975).

Chapter 6

1. Elkind, *Children and Adolescents,* p. 6.
2. See John Stevens Kerr, ed., *Teaching Grades Seven through Ten* (Philadelphia: Parish Life Press, 1980), Part III.
3. On using parables with youth see A. Roger Gobbel, Gertrude G. Gobbel, and Thomas Ridenhour Sr., *Helping Youth Interpret the Bible* (Atlanta: John Knox Press, 1984), pp. 113-117, 137-139.

4. A helpful book on this subject is Charles M. Shelton, *Adolescent Spirituality: Pastoral Ministry for High School and College Youth* (Chicago: Loyola University Press, 1983). See especially Chapter 4.

5. David Elkind, *All Grown Up and No Place to Go: Teenagers in Crisis* (Reading, Mass.: Addison-Wesley Publishing Co., 1984), Chapter 3.

6. On peers, see Elkind, *Sympathetic Understanding*, pp. 154ff; and Arthur T. Jersild, Judith S. Brook, and David W. Brook, *Psychology of Adolescence*, 3rd ed. (New York: Macmillan Publishing Co., 1978), Chapter 13.

7. Elkind, *All Grown Up*, Chapter 4.

8. Jersild, Brook, and Brook, *Adolescence*, p. 304.

9. See Elkind, *All Grown Up*, pp. 116-120.

10. See ibid., Chapter 5.

11. Ibid., p. 33.

12. Ibid., pp. 4-15. Also see David Elkind, *The Hurried Child: Growing Up Too Fast Too Soon* (Reading, Mass.: Addison-Wesley Publishing Co., 1981), Chapters 1-4, 7.

13. Elkind, *All Grown Up*, Chapters 4, 6, 7.

Chapter 7

1. Gerhard O. Forde comments graphically on our human inclination in *Justification by Faith—A Matter of Death and Life* (Philadelphia: Fortress Press, 1982), pp. 22-23, 37-38.

2. For an excellent study of justification see John Reumann, *"Righteousness" in the New Testament: Justification in the United States Lutheran-Roman Catholic Dialogue* (Philadelphia: Fortress Press, 1982); Chapter 3 may be particularly useful. Also see Foster R. McCurley and John Reumann, *Witness of the Word: A Biblical Theology of the Gospel* (Philadelphia: Fortress Press, 1986), pp. 338-343.

3. For further characteristics of adults and general implications for teaching, see Marvin L. Roloff, ed., *Education for Christian Living* (Minneapolis: Augsburg Publishing House, 1987), pp. 133-138.

4. Elkind, *All Grown Up*, pp. 31-32.

5. Tillich, *Systematic Theology*, 2:78.

6. On loneliness as part of the human *question*, see Tillich's distinction between solitude and loneliness in ibid., pp. 82-83.

7. Ibid., pp. 200-203.

8. W.H.C. Frend, *The Rise of Christianity* (Philadelphia: Fortress Press, 1984), pp. 673-679. Frend is a good resource to help adults learn about the early church struggles on many issues.

9. See Walther von Loewenich, *Luther's Theology of the Cross*, trans. Herbert J. A. Bouman (Minneapolis: Augsburg Publishing House, 1976), pp. 117-123.

10. See Sharon Parks, *The Critical Years: The Young Adult Search for a Faith to Live By* (San Francisco: Harper and Row, 1986), pp. 86-88. On mentoring, also see Daniel J. Levinson et al., *The Seasons of a Man's Life* (New York: Alfred A. Knopf, 1978), pp. 97-101.
11. Althaus, *Theology of Martin Luther,* p. 408.
12. Levinson, *Seasons,* pp. 245-251, and Gail Sheehy, *Passages: Predictable Crises of Adult Life* (New York: Bantam Books ed., 1977), pp. 356-357.
13. For an excellent summary of theories of adult development from which you can draw many implications for teaching, see Robert F. Rodgers, "Theories of Adult Development: Research Status and Counseling Implications" in Steven D. Brown and Robert W. Lent, *Handbook of Counseling Psychology* (New York: John Wiley and Sons, 1984), pp. 479-519.
14. Stanley Hauerwas, "Character, Narrative, and Growth in the Christian Life" in Brusselmans, *Toward Moral and Religious Maturity,* p. 447.
15. Ibid. For Hauerwas's detailed analysis of the self and the development of character, see Stanley Hauerwas, *Character and the Christian Life: A Study in Theological Ethics* (San Antonio: Trinity University Press, 1975), *passim.*
16. Hauerwas in Brusselmans, *Toward Moral and Religious Maturity,* p. 452.
17. Ibid., pp. 447, 452.
18. Ibid., p. 461.
19. Ibid., p. 465.
20. Ibid., p. 468. Cf. George W. Stroup (*The Promise of Narrative Theology: Recovering the Gospel in the Church* [Atlanta: John Knox Press, 1981], p. 171) who says that, in the light of the Christian narratives, personal history can be reinterpreted, identities and even worlds may be altered, and reality perceived in a radically new way.
21. Hauerwas in Brusselmans, *Toward Moral and Religious Maturity,* p. 471.
22. Ibid., pp. 471-472.
23. Stephen Crites, "The Narrative Quality of Experience," *Journal of the American Academy of Religion* 39 (1971): 291.
24. Ibid., p. 294.
25. Ibid., p. 296.
26. Ibid., p. 297.
27. Ibid., p. 306.
28. See Stephen Brookfield, *Adult Learners, Adult Education and the Community* (New York: Teachers College Press, 1984), pp. 150-154. Also see Leon McKenzie, *The Religious Education of Adults* (Birmingham, Ala.: Religious Education Press, 1982), pp. 130-131, and Linda Jane Vogel, *The Religious Education of Older Adults* (Birmingham, Ala.: Religious Education Press, 1984), pp. 113-115.
29. Cf. Dick Murray, *Strengthening the Adult Sunday School Class* (Nashville: Abingdon Press, 1981), pp. 34-43.

Chapter 8

1. See Richard M. Restak, *The Brain: The Last Frontier* (Garden City, N.Y.: Doubleday and Co., 1979), pp. 168, 172. Also see Daniel C. Batson and

W. Larry Ventnis, *The Religious Experience: A Social Psychological Perspective* (New York: Oxford University Press, 1982), pp. 79-80.

2. See articles by Paul E. Bumbar, Carla de Sola and Arthur Easton, Michael G. Lawler, and Andrew D. Thompson in Gloria Durka and Joanmarie Smith, eds., *Aesthetic Dimensions of Religious Education* (New York: Paulist Press, 1979).

3. Batson and Ventnis, *Religious Experience,* pp. 65-79.

4. Ibid., p. 80.

5. Ibid., p. 81-87.

6. Ibid., p. 87. Also, Guilford asserts that there are two abilities for creative thinking—the generation of a variety of ideas and transformation abilities which produce new patterns and forms. Guilford is particularly intrigued by the period of incubation in the process. (Harold W. Bernard and Wesley C. Huckins, eds., *Exploring Human Development: Interdisciplinary Readings* [Boston: Allyn and Bacon, 1972], p. 203).

7. Batson and Ventnis, *Religious Experience,* p. 87.

8. See Amos N. Wilder, "Story and Story World," *Interpretation* 37 (October 1983): 353-364.

9. See James E. Loder, "Creativity in and Beyond Human Development" in Durka and Smith, *Aesthetic Dimensions,* pp. 219ff.

10. In therapeutic work, Richard Gardiner's acceptance of the child's own stories is a factor in the child's learning and growth. The therapist's acceptance leads to the child's self-perception of the need for change. We might see in such acceptance an analog (human, and therefore ambiguous) to the unconditional acceptance that opens up to us our unacceptableness and provides the possibility of new life.

11. Paul Tillich, "Creative Love in Education," *World Christian Education* 18:3 (third quarter, 1963): 70, 75.

12. George Lindbeck points to the importance of ritual, prayer, and example in the learning process. He says, "The aesthetic and nondiscursively symbolic dimensions of a religion—for example, its poetry, music, art, and rituals—are not . . . mere decorations. . . . Rather, it is through these that the basic patterns of religion are interiorized, exhibited and transmitted." (*The Nature of Doctrine: Religion and Theology in a Post-liberal Age* [Philadelphia: Westminster Press, 1984], pp. 35-36.)

13. Cf. James Michael Lee, *The Shape of Religious Instruction* (Mishawaka, Ind.: Religious Education Press, 1971), pp. 2-3; James Michael Lee, "The Authentic Source of Religious Instruction" in Norma H. Thompson, *Religious Education and Theology* (Birmingham, Ala.: Religious Education Press, 1982), pp. 146, 150, 155; and James Michael Lee, ed., *The Religious Education We Need: Toward the Renewal of Christian Education* (Mishawaka, Ind.: Religious Education Press, 1977), p. 121.

14. Cf. James D. Smart, *The Teaching Ministry of the Church* (Philadelphia: Westminster Press, 1954) tends to give this impression. In his approach,

the emphasis is on the biblical witness to revelation, rather than, say, psychological information about the learner or new procedures. Not that Smart would ignore the latter; but they are not his primary concern in religious education.

15. For the praxis-reflection model, see Paolo Freire, *Pedagogy of the Oppressed*, trans. Myna Bergman Ramos (New York: Seabury Press, 1968) and Thomas H. Groome, *Christian Religious Education: Sharing Our Story and Vision* (San Francisco: Harper and Row, 1980).

Appendix

1. The interpretation of this story reflects Loder's analysis, *Transforming Moment*, pp. 96ff.